FREE Study Skills DVD Offer

Dear Customer,

Thank you for your purchase from Mometrix! We consider it an honor and a privilege that you have purchased our product and we want to ensure your satisfaction.

As a way of showing our appreciation and to help us better serve you, we have developed a Study Skills DVD that we would like to give you for <u>FREE</u>. This DVD covers our *best practices* for getting ready for your exam, from how to use our study materials to how to best prepare for the day of the test.

All that we ask is that you email us with feedback that would describe your experience so far with our product. Good, bad, or indifferent, we want to know what you think!

To get your FREE Study Skills DVD, email <u>freedvd@mometrix.com</u> with *FREE STUDY SKILLS DVD* in the subject line and the following information in the body of the email:

- The name of the product you purchased.
- Your product rating on a scale of 1-5, with 5 being the highest rating.
- Your feedback. It can be long, short, or anything in between. We just want to know your impressions and experience so far with our product. (Good feedback might include how our study material met your needs and ways we might be able to make it even better. You could highlight features that you found helpful or features that you think we should add.)
- Your full name and shipping address where you would like us to send your free DVD.

If you have any questions or concerns, please don't hesitate to contact me directly.

Thanks again!

Sincerely,

Jay Willis
Vice President
<u>jay.willis@mometrix.com</u>
1-800-673-8175

ACCUPLACER
Practice Test Book
2019-2020

Two Full-Length ACCUPLACER Practice Tests with Math, Reading, and Writing

Written and edited by the Mometrix College Placement Test Team

Printed in the United States of America

This paper meets the requirements of ANSI/NISO Z39.48-1992 (Permanence of Paper).

Mometrix offers volume discount pricing to institutions. For more information or a price quote, please contact our sales department at sales@mometrix.com or 888-248-1219.

Paperback
ISBN 13: 978-1-5167-1220-5
ISBN 10: 1-5167-1220-X

DEAR FUTURE EXAM SUCCESS STORY

First of all, **THANK YOU** for purchasing Mometrix study materials!

Second, congratulations! You are one of the few determined test-takers who are committed to doing whatever it takes to excel on your exam. **You have come to the right place.** We developed these practice tests with one goal in mind: to deliver you the best possible approximation of the questions you will see on test day.

Standardized testing is one of the biggest obstacles on your road to success, which only increases the importance of doing well in the high-pressure, high-stakes environment of test day. Your results on this test could have a significant impact on your future, and these practice tests will give you the repetitions you need to build your familiarity and confidence with the test content and format to help you achieve your full potential on test day.

Your success is our success

We would love to hear from you! If you would like to share the story of your exam success or if you have any questions or comments in regard to our products, please contact us at **800-673-8175** or **support@mometrix.com**.

Thanks again for your business and we wish you continued success!

Sincerely,
The Mometrix Test Preparation Team

TABLE OF CONTENTS

Practice Test #1

SENTENCE SKILLS

Sentence Correction

Directions for questions 1–10

Select the best version of the underlined part of the sentence. The first choice is the same as the original sentence. If you think the original sentence is best, choose the first answer.

1. Children who aren't nurtured during infancy are more likely to develop attachment disorders, <u>which can cause persisting and severely problems</u> later in life.

    A. which can cause persisting and severely problems
    B. that can cause persisting and severe problem
    C. they can cause persistent and severe problem
    D. which can cause persistent and severe problems

2. While speed is a measure of how fast an object is moving, velocity measures how fast an object is moving <u>and also indicates in what direction</u> it is traveling.

    A. and also indicates in what direction
    B. and only indicates in which direction
    C. and also indicate in which directions
    D. and only indicated in what direction

3. Many companies are now using social networking sites like Facebook and MySpace <u>to market there service and product.</u>

    A. to market there service and product
    B. to market their services and products
    C. and market their service and products
    D. which market their services and products

4. An autoclave is a tool used mainly in hospitals <u>to sterilizing surgical tools and hypodermic needles.</u>

    A. to sterilizing surgical tools and hypodermic needles
    B. for sterilize surgical tools and hypodermic needles
    C. to sterilize surgical tools and hypodermic needles
    D. for sterilizing the surgical tool and hypodermic needle

5. <u>The bizarre creatures known by electric eels</u> are capable of emitting an incredible 600 volts of electricity.

    A. The bizarre creatures known by electric eels
    B. A bizarre creature known as electric eels
    C. The bizarre creatures known to electric eels
    D. The bizarre creatures known as electric eels

1

6. <u>A key factor taken into account during city planning is</u> where major services and amenities will be located.

    A. A key factor taken into account during city planning is
    B. Key factors taken into account during city planning is
    C. A key factor taking into account during city planning is
    D. Key factors, taken into accounting during city planning are

7. Jupiter with its numerous moons, and Great Red Spot, has been studied extensively by astronomers.

    A. Jupiter with its numerous moons, and Great Red Spot,
    B. Jupiter with, its numerous moons and Great Red Spot,
    C. Jupiter, with its numerous moons and Great Red Spot,
    D. Jupiter with, its numerous moons, and Great Red Spot,

8. Many gardeners are now making their own backyard compost, which is not only cheap, but also helps to cut down on landfill waste.

    A. which is not only cheap, but also helps to cut down on landfill waste
    B. which is not only cheaper, but also cuts down on landfill's waste
    C. which is, not only cheap, but also, helps to cut down on landfill waste
    D. which is not only done cheaply, but is also cutting down on landfills wastes

9. <u>The growth of the security industry can be large attributable</u> to the fact that people are less trusting of others than they once were.

    A. The growth of the security industry can be large attributable
    B. The growing of the securities industry can be largely attributable
    C. The growth on the security industry can be large attributed
    D. The growth of the security industry can be largely attributed

10. Claude Monet was a famous painter <u>who's well-known painting includes</u> *San Giorgio Maggiore at Dusk* and *The Water Lily Pond*.

    A. who's well-known painting includes
    B. whose well-known painting including
    C. whose well-known paintings include
    D. who well-known paintings include

Construction Shift

Directions for questions 11–20

Rewrite the sentence in your head following the directions given below. Keep in mind that your new sentence should be well written and should have essentially the same meaning as the original sentence.

11. Bats and dolphins use a process known as echolocation, which means they emit and receive frequencies that can help them navigate through the dark night and murky waters, and also allows them to locate food sources like insects or fish.

Rewrite, beginning with

　　　　Locating food sources like insects or fish

The next words will be

　　A. during which they emit and receive frequencies
　　B. is done through a process known as echolocation
　　C. helps them navigate through the dark night
　　D. is done by bats and dolphins

12. Carbon dating is an accepted method used by archaeologists to figure out the age of artifacts, even though it may not be entirely accurate if samples are contaminated or if the objects to be dated are not extremely old.

Rewrite, beginning with

　　　　Even though carbon dating is not always entirely accurate,

The next words will be

　　A. it is an accepted method
　　B. objects to be dated
　　C. to figure out the age
　　D. samples are contaminated

13. Chemical changes are sometimes difficult to distinguish from physical changes, but some examples of physical changes, such as melting water, chopped wood, and ripped paper, are very easy to recognize.

Rewrite, beginning with

　　　　Melting water, chopped wood, and ripped paper

The next words will be

　　A. are sometimes difficult to distinguish
　　B. are very easy to recognize
　　C. are chemical changes
　　D. are some examples of physical changes

14. The theory of repressed memory was developed by Sigmund Freud, and it stated that all people store memories that cannot be accessed during daily life, but can be accessed through hypnotherapy and hypnosis.

Rewrite, beginning with

Developed by Sigmund Freud,

The next words will be

A. it stated that all people
B. that cannot be accessed
C. hypnotherapy and hypnosis
D. the theory of repressed memory

15. Romantic poetry is an important genre, and the works are easily distinguished from other types of poetry by a few characteristics, including their focus on nature and the importance that is ascribed to everyday occurrences.

Rewrite, beginning with

A focus on nature and the importance that is ascribed to everyday occurrences

The next words will be

A. are easily distinguished
B. from other types of poetry
C. are a few characteristics
D. is an important genre

16. The Sugar Act was implemented in 1764 by England, and it required individuals residing in the colonies of the United States to pay a tax on sugar, as well as on dyes and other goods.

Rewrite, beginning with

Implemented in 1764 by England

The next words will be

A. the Sugar Act
B. it required individuals
C. in the colonies
D. on sugar

17. Oil spill, as the phrase suggests, refers to the accidental introduction of oil into environments, and even though it can refer to land spills, the phrase is usually understood to refer to spills in water.

Rewrite, beginning with

Even though the phrase "oil spill" is usually understood to refer to spills in water

The next words will be

A. as the name suggests
B. it can refer to land spills
C. and the introduction of oil
D. known as oil spills

18. Radar was first used in 1904, and at that time all it was capable of was determining whether objects were present, but now it can determine the size and shape of an object, among other things, as well.

Rewrite, beginning with

Although once only capable of determining the presence of objects,

The next words will be

    A. radar was first used
    B. among other things
    C. radar can now determine
    D. the size and shape of an object

19. Placebos are often used in drug studies, and the effectiveness of a drug can be determined by measuring whether people with illnesses or diseases show significantly more improvement when they are given a real drug rather than a placebo.

Rewrite, beginning with

By measuring whether people with illnesses show significantly more improvement when given a real drug,

The next words will be

    A. the effectiveness of a drug
    B. placebos can be used in drug studies
    C. it is rather than a placebo
    D. is often used in drug studies

20. Employees value salary and good benefits in a job, but many also consider having an enjoyable job important, so it's difficult to say what the majority of people value most in a career.

Rewrite, beginning with

While many people consider having an enjoyable job important,

The next words will be

    A. it's what the majority of people
    B. it's difficult to say
    C. salary and good benefits
    D. other employees value

READING COMPREHENSION

Directions for questions 1–10

Read the statement or passage and then choose the best answer to the question. Answer the question based on what is stated or implied in the statement or passage.

1. The Amazon Rainforest is one of the most important ecosystems in the world. However, it is slowly being destroyed. Areas of the rainforest are being cleared for farms and roads, and much of the wood is also being harvested and sold. There are several compelling reasons to protect this area. First, a significant number of pharmaceuticals are made from plants that have been discovered in the rainforest, and it's quite possible there are still important plants that have not yet been discovered. Secondly, the rainforest provides a significant portion of the world's oxygen and also absorbs great amounts of carbon dioxide. Without rainforests, global warming could accelerate.

The main purpose of the passage is

    A. to present the major reasons why the Amazon Rainforest is being destroyed.
    B. to explain why the Amazon Rainforest should be protected.
    C. to argue that rainforest destruction is a major cause of global warming.
    D. to discuss how the rainforest has helped in the development of medications.

2. Howard Gardner was a psychologist best known for developing the theory of multiple intelligences. Basically, the theory states that the idea of general intelligence or overall intelligence is somewhat inaccurate. This is because people often show intelligence in different areas. He argued that there are actually different types of intelligence. One type of intelligence that Gardner identified was interpersonal intelligence. People who possess this type of intelligence relate and interact well with others. Intrapersonal intelligence, on the other hand, implies that people are in touch with their own feelings. They enjoy thinking about theories and developing their own thoughts and ideas. People who have linguistic intelligence learn best by taking notes and reading textbooks. These people usually excel in traditional academic environments, as many academic subjects stress these types of activities. The other types of intelligence are kinesthetic, musical, spatial, and logical/mathematical.

We can conclude from the passage that

    A. Gardner believed that linguistic intelligence was the most desirable type to have.
    B. most people who have a high level of intrapersonal intelligence do well in school.
    C. people who have a high level of interpersonal intelligence work well in groups.
    D. people who have mathematical intelligence would do the best on a standard IQ test.

3. The Internet has made life a whole lot easier for many people, but being online also brings with it very real risks. Hackers can steal personal and financial information. There are several precautions that computer users can take to minimize the level of risk that is involved with being online. One of the most obvious safety precautions is to purchase a good anti-virus and anti-spyware program. Passwords are also a very important part of online security, and several tips can help users create more secure passwords. First, they should be something that can easily be remembered, but they shouldn't be something others can guess easily. Your first or last name, phone number, or the name of your street are all bad choices, as people could learn this information quite easily. Longer passwords are more secure, and those that use a mixture of upper and lower case letters and a combination of letters and numbers are more secure than those that don't. Finally, passwords should be changed often. This can make remembering them more difficult, but the extra effort is worth the added security.

The main purpose of this passage is to

A. discuss the major risks associated with Internet use.
B. talk about the importance of anti-virus programs.
C. outline important considerations for passwords.
D. discuss why certain types of passwords shouldn't be used.

4. When people are conducting research, particularly historical research, they usually rely on primary and secondary sources. Primary sources are the more direct type of information. They are accounts of an event that are produced by individuals who were actually present. Some examples of primary sources include a person's diary entry about an event, an interview with an eyewitness, a newspaper article, or a transcribed conversation. Secondary sources are pieces of information that are constructed through the use of other, primary sources. Often, the person who creates the secondary source was not actually present at the event. Secondary sources could include books, research papers, and magazine articles.

From the passage it can be assumed that

A. primary sources are easier to find than secondary sources.
B. primary sources provide more accurate information than secondary sources.
C. secondary sources give more accurate information than primary sources.
D. secondary sources are always used when books or articles are being written.

5. Many people fail to realize just how crucial getting a good night's sleep actually is. It is usually suggested that adults get about seven hours of sleep every night, and younger children should get even more. Sleep has several benefits. First, it is believed to improve memory. This is one reason why it is always preferable to sleep the night before a test rather than stay up for the entire night to review the information. On a related note, sleep also improves concentration and mental alertness. Those who get sufficient sleep are able to concentrate on work tasks better and also react faster when they are driving a car, for example. Finally, people who get enough sleep have better immunity against illness. The reason for this is not fully understood, but researchers believe that an increase in the production of growth hormone and melatonin plays a role.

The main purpose of this passage is

A. to talk about the benefits of sleep.
B. to discuss how much sleep people should get.
C. to identify which hormones can boost immunity.
D. to present strategies for improving memory and concentration.

6. Feudalism was a type of social system that existed in parts of Europe during the Middle Ages. Essentially, there were several different classes within a feudal society. The king controlled all of the land in his jurisdiction. He divided this land among a few barons. The barons then divided up the land they were given and distributed it to knights. It was then split up again and distributed to serfs, who were the lowest members of feudal society. They were permitted to farm a small section of land, but they had to give a portion of their food to the knights in exchange for this privilege. They also had to give free labor to the knights who allowed them to use their land. Serfs had very few rights; they weren't even allowed to leave their land without permission from the knight who controlled the land. The system of feudalism ended when money began to be used as currency instead of land.

It can be concluded that

    A. serfs were in a better position when the economy changed to a money-based one.

    B. there were more knights in a typical feudal society than barons.

    C. the knights did not have to do anything for the barons in exchange for land.

    D. most feudal societies in Europe were ruled by more than one king.

7. A bird's feathers are extremely important, and when they clean and smooth them, it is known as preening. Birds in the wild preen their feathers on a regular basis. This is true of most captive birds as well, but not all. For example, some birds do not preen their feathers at all. This problem is most common in birds that are taken from their mothers at a very young age. Presumably, the absence of preening is due to the fact that they were never shown how to do it properly. A more common problem among captive birds is excessive preening. Some birds may pull out large numbers of their feathers or bite them down to the skin. It should be noted that wild birds never exhibit this kind of behavior. There are several suggestions about how the problem of excessive preening can be solved. Giving birds baths or placing them in an area that has more activity to prevent boredom are suggestions. However, these measures are often not sufficient to solve the problem.

The purpose of the passage is

    A. to give an overview of abnormal preening in birds.

    B. to compare captive birds to wild birds.

    C. to discuss why preening is important.

    D. to explain how excessive preening problems can be solved.

8. Hibernation in animals is an extremely fascinating phenomenon, one that biologists are not yet close to understanding fully. However, it is quite easy to understand why animals hibernate during the cold winter months. Usually, it is because their food is quite scarce during this time. Animals that are herbivores will find the winters extremely tough, because all of the vegetation will have died off by the time winter arrives. Hibernation is essentially a way of dealing with this food shortage. Animals like birds rely on seeds and small insects for sustenance. Obviously, these will also be quite scarce in the winter when the ground becomes covered and frozen. Many birds address their upcoming food shortage in quite a different way: they migrate to warmer areas where their sources of food will be plentiful.

The main reason animals hibernate is

    A. to travel to a warmer area where food will be more plentiful.

    B. to cut down on their food consumption during the winter months.

    C. to avoid the harsh weather that occurs during the winter months.

    D. to avoid food shortages that occur during the winter months.

9. At one time, the use of leeches to treat medical problems was quite common. If a person suffered from a snake bite or a bee sting, leeches were believed to be capable of removing the poison from the body if they were placed on top of the wound. They have also been used for blood letting and to stop hemorrhages, although neither of these leech treatments would be considered acceptable by present-day physicians. Today, leeches are still used on a limited basis. Most often, leeches are used to drain blood from clogged veins. This results in little pain for the patient and also ensures the patient's blood will not clot while it is being drained.

The main purpose of the passage is

    A. to discuss the benefits of using leeches to treat blocked veins.
    B. to give an overview of how leeches have been used throughout history.
    C. to compare which uses of leeches are effective and which are not.
    D. to explain how leeches can be used to remove poison from the body.

10. When online file-sharing programs emerged, the music industry changed forever. Perhaps the first widely-used music file sharing program was Napster. It allowed users to sign up to use the service at no charge. Then, they could download music files from other users all over the world by simply typing in what song or album they wanted. Obviously, this was bad news for music artists and record labels because they weren't making any profits from downloaded music. Eventually, Napster was shut down. While it later reinvented itself as a paying service, other free music-sharing sites cropped up almost immediately. Even though several sites and individual users have been charged, there are still countless individuals who log onto these sites to obtain free music.

The main problem associated with peer file-sharing sites is

    A. it is hard to locate users to criminally charge them.
    B. there are too many of them currently in existence.
    C. they prevent artists and labels from earning money.
    D. they allow users to sign up for the service free of charge.

Directions for questions 11–20

For the questions that follow, two underlined sentences are followed by a question or statement. Read the sentences, then choose the best answer to the question or the best completion of the statement.

11. **Zoos are places that serve no other purpose than to allow greedy owners to make money.**
    Some of the world's most endangered animals can be found in zoos, where they are protected from poachers and predators.

What does the second sentence do?

    A. It challenges the first.
    B. It provides an example.
    C. It supports the first.
    D. It restates the first.

12. Elephants are highly intelligent animals that are known to display several human-like behaviors.

> When a member of their herd dies, elephants create graves for their fallen comrades, and have been known to visit burial sites years after the elephant's death.

What does the second sentence do?

    A. It provides a contrast.
    B. It provides an example.
    C. It restates the information from the first.
    D. It offers a solution.

13. Aerobic exercises, which include biking and running, offer several benefits, including better cardiovascular health.

> Those who regularly walk or do other forms of aerobic exercise typically have a lower resting heart rate and suffer fewer heart problems.

What does the second sentence do?

    A. It offers a solution.
    B. It presents an example.
    C. It contradicts the information in the first.
    D. It expands on the information in the first.

14. Despite advancements in contraceptive technologies, teen pregnancy is still a huge problem in the United States.

> Many schools are choosing not to teach students about contraception, and that means many may not be aware of how to obtain effective contraceptives.

What does the second sentence do?

    A. It expands on the information in the first.
    B. It offers a solution.
    C. It provides an explanation.
    D. It restates the information in the first.

15. Although it may seem impossible, solving a Rubik's Cube is quite doable if one knows about the various solving methods.

> Manipulating the cube so that all of the corner pieces are in their correct positions and then essentially filling in the blanks is a time-consuming but effective solving method.

What does the second sentence do?

    A. It contrasts with the first.
    B. It offers an explanation.
    C. It restates the information in the first.
    D. It expands on the information in the first.

16. Many people now use digital devices such as PDAs to keep track of their schedules.

   PDAs are easy to use and, unlike day planners, there is no need to carry around a bulky notebook or search for a pen when you need to add something.

How are the sentences related?

   A. They provide a statement and an explanation.
   B. They present a problem and a possible solution.
   C. They present a principle and an example.
   D. They contradict each other.

17. DDT is a pesticide that is thought to adversely affect bird populations and contribute to the incidence of cancer in humans.

   In 1972, the use of DDT in the United States was banned.

What does the second sentence do?

   A. It supports the first.
   B. It states a result.
   C. It gives an example.
   D. It provides an explanation.

18. People who are concerned about the very real and sometimes serious side effects of conventional drugs are now turning to natural remedies.

   Natural remedies offer an alternative to drugs prescribed by doctors, which can often have serious adverse effects.

How are the two sentences related?

   A. They contradict each other.
   B. They support each other.
   C. They repeat the same information.
   D. They present a cause and an effect.

19. Students should study what they are passionate about when they attend university.

   Any individual considering university should research the job market and make decisions about what they will study based on current employment trends.

What does the second sentence do?

   A. It contradicts the first.
   B. It provides an example.
   C. It expands on the first.
   D. It offers a solution.

20. Biological weapons, although considered by many to be relatively new, have actually been used by militaries for thousands of years.

   In Greece, one military used biological warfare by throwing venomous snakes onto the ship of their enemy.

What does the second sentence do?

   A. It offers a solution.
   B. It provides an example.
   C. It contradicts the first.
   D. It presents an effect.

ARITHMETIC

Solve the following problems and select your answer from the choices given. You may use the paper you have been given for scratch paper.

1. Which of the following is equivalent to $\frac{27}{8}$?

- A. $2\frac{7}{8}$
- B. $3\frac{3}{8}$
- C. $4\frac{5}{8}$
- D. $9\frac{3}{8}$

2. $6.32 - 3.5 =$

- A. 2.82
- B. 3.18
- C. 3.27
- D. 5.97

3. A box is 30 cm long, 20 cm wide, and 15 cm high. What is the volume of the box?

- A. 65 cm^3
- B. 260 cm^3
- C. 1,125 cm^3
- D. 9,000 cm^3

4. 9.5% of the people in a town voted for a certain proposition in a municipal election. If the town's population is 51,623, about how many people in the town voted for the proposition?

- A. 3,000
- B. 5,000
- C. 7,000
- D. 10,000

5. What is $\frac{5}{6}$ of $\frac{3}{4}$?

- A. $\frac{2}{3}$
- B. $\frac{3}{5}$
- C. $\frac{4}{5}$
- D. $\frac{5}{8}$

6. There are twelve inches in a foot, and three feet in a yard. How many inches are in five yards?

- A. 20
- B. 41
- C. 75
- D. 180

7. $2.2 \times 31.3 =$

    A. 6.886

    B. 68.86

    C. 688.6

    D. 6886.00

8. What is the average of $\frac{1}{3}, \frac{2}{3}$**, and** $\frac{1}{4}$**?**

    A. $\frac{1}{2}$

    B. $\frac{2}{5}$

    C. $\frac{3}{8}$

    D. $\frac{5}{12}$

9. Which of the following is equal to 0.0023**?**

    A. 2.3×10^{-3}

    B. 2.3×10^{-2}

    C. 2.3×10^{2}

    D. 2.3×10^{3}

10. A reporter for a school newspaper surveys the students at the school to ask if they prefer chocolate, vanilla, or strawberry ice cream. Of the students who answer her question, 35% prefer vanilla, and 40% prefer chocolate. What percent of the students she surveyed prefer strawberry?

    A. 15%

    B. 25%

    C. 45%

    D. There is not enough information to say.

11. A cookie recipe calls for $2\frac{1}{4}$ **cups of milk. Brian has** $1\frac{1}{2}$ **cups available. How much more milk does he need in order to make cookies according to the recipe?**

    A. $1\frac{1}{2}$ cups

    B. $1\frac{1}{4}$ cups

    C. $\frac{3}{4}$ cup

    D. $\frac{1}{4}$ cup

12. Which of the following fractions is closest to $\frac{15,012}{19,938}$ **?**

    A. $\frac{1}{4}$

    B. $\frac{3}{4}$

    C. $\frac{4}{5}$

    D. $\frac{5}{9}$

13. $\frac{2}{5} \times 2.5 =$

A. 1

B. 2

C. 4

D. 6

14. Sam runs for fifteen minutes at eight miles per hour, and then jogs for forty-five minutes at four miles per hour. What is his average speed during this time?

A. 5 miles per hour

B. 5.5 miles per hour

C. 6 miles per hour

D. 7 miles per hour

15. In the diagram below, all five angles are equal. What is the measure of each angle?

A. 20°

B. 36°

C. 60°

D. 72°

16. What percent of 800 is 40?

A. 2%

B. 5%

C. 20%

D. 32%

17. $\frac{3}{16} =$

A. 0.025

B. 0.533

C. 0.1875

D. 0.2025

ELEMENTARY ALGEBRA

Solve the following problems and select your answer from the choices given. You may use the paper you have been given for scratch paper.

18. Which of the following is equivalent to $3 - 2x < 5$?

A. $x < 1$
B. $x > 1$
C. $x < -1$
D. $x > -1$

19. $6\left(-\frac{2}{3}\right) - 2\left(-\frac{7}{2}\right) =$

A. -9
B. -4
C. 3
D. 4

20. Which of the following is equivalent to $\left(\sqrt[3]{x^4}\right)^5$?

A. $x^{\frac{12}{5}}$
B. $x^{\frac{15}{4}}$
C. $x^{\frac{20}{3}}$
D. x^{60}

21. If $x > 2$, then $\left(\frac{x^2-5x+6}{x+1}\right) \times \left(\frac{x+1}{x-2}\right) =$

A. $x + 1$
B. $x - 3$
C. $\frac{x^2+2x+1}{x-2}$
D. $\frac{x^2-2x-3}{x+1}$

22. $|x| > x$ for what values of x?

A. $x < 0$
B. $x > 0$
C. $|x| > x$ for all real values of x.
D. There is no real number x such that $|x| > x$.

23. $\left(\sqrt{2} + \sqrt{3}\right) \times \left(2 + \sqrt{6}\right) = ?$

A. $2\sqrt{6} + 4$
B. $3\sqrt{2} + 2\sqrt{3}$
C. $5\sqrt{2} + 4\sqrt{3}$
D. $2\sqrt{5} + \sqrt{30}$

24. The formula for the volume of a pyramid is $\frac{1}{3}Bh$, where B is the area of the base and h is the height. The Pyramid of Khafre in Giza has a square base about 700 feet on a side and is about 450 feet high. Which of the following is closest to its volume?

    A. 18 million cubic feet
    B. 55 million cubic feet
    C. 75 million cubic feet
    D. 220 million cubic feet

25. What is $\frac{x^3+2x}{x+3}$ when $= -1$?

    A. $-\frac{3}{2}$
    B. $-\frac{2}{3}$
    C. $\frac{1}{2}$
    D $\frac{3}{4}$

26. A certain exam has 30 questions. A student gets 1 point for each question he gets right and loses half a point for a question he answers incorrectly; he neither gains nor loses any points for a question left blank. If C is the number of questions a student gets right and B is the number of questions he leaves blank, which of the following represents his score on the exam?

    A. $C - \frac{1}{2}B$
    B. $C - \frac{1}{2}(30 - B)$
    C. $C - \frac{1}{2}(30 - B - C)$
    D. $(30 - C) - \frac{1}{2}(30 - B)$

27. $\frac{|2|+|-2|}{|3|-|-1|} =$

    A. 0
    B. 1
    C. 2
    D. 4

28. $\frac{x^2}{y^2} + \frac{x}{y^3} =$

    A. $\frac{x^3+x}{y^3}$
    B. $\frac{x^2+xy}{y^3}$
    C. $\frac{x^2y+xy}{y^3}$
    D. $\frac{x^2y+x}{y^3}$

29. Every person attending a certain meeting hands out a business card to every other person at the meeting. If there are a total of 30 cards handed out, how many people are at the meeting?

    A. 5
    B. 6
    C. 10
    D. 15

COLLEGE-LEVEL MATH

Solve the following problems and select your answer from the choices given. You may use the paper you have been given for scratch paper.

30. What is the area of a parallelogram with vertices $(0, 0)$, $(4, 5)$, $(10, 7)$, and $(6, 2)$?

    A. 20
    B. 22
    C. 24
    D. 26
    E. 28

31. If $3^x = 2$, then $x =$

    A. 9
    B. $\sqrt{3}$
    C. $\sqrt[3]{2}$
    D. $\log_3 2$
    E. $\log_2 3$

32. Which of these is described by the equation $9x^2 + 6xy + y^2 - 5x + y = 13$?

    A. An ellipse
    B. A parabola
    C. A hyperbola
    D. A spiral
    E. Two parallel lines

33. If $f(x) = \tan(2x + 4)$, then $f^{-1}(x) =$

    A. $\tan^{-1}(2x + 4)$
    B. $\sec(2x + 4)$
    C. $\tan^{-1}\left(\frac{1}{2}x - 2\right)$
    D. $2\tan^{-1}(x) - 4$
    E. $\frac{1}{2}\tan^{-1}(x) - 2$

34. $\sqrt[5]{\left(\sqrt[8]{9^{10}}\right)^6} =$

    A. 1
    B. 3
    C. $3\sqrt{3}$
    D. 27
    E. 81

35. $|6 + 2i| =$

    A. $2\sqrt{3}$

    B. $2\sqrt{10}$

    C. 6

    D. 8

    E. 12

36. A certain rectangular room is twice as wide as it is tall, and three times as long as it is wide. If the room has a volume of 12,000 ft³, what is its width?

    A. 10 ft.

    B. 12 ft.

    C. 20 ft.

    D. 30 ft.

    E. $10\sqrt[3]{12}$ ft.

37. When $(a + 2b)^5$ is expanded into a polynomial, which of the following terms does *not* appear?

    A. a^5

    B. $10a^4b$

    C. $32b^5$

    D. $40ab^4$

    E. $80a^2b^3$

38. Which of the following is equivalent to $\ln 7 + \ln 5 - \ln 3$?

    A. $\ln 4$

    B. $\ln 9$

    C. $\ln \frac{35}{3}$

    D. $\log_3 12$

    E. $\log_7 2$

39. If $\sec \theta = 2$, then which of the following is a possible value for $\sin \theta$?

    A. $-\frac{\sqrt{3}}{2}$

    B. $-\frac{1}{2}$

    C. 0

    D. 1

    E. $\frac{\sqrt{2}}{2}$

40. Which of the following is the correct graph of the system of inequalities below?

$$x - y > 1$$
$$2x + y > 2$$

a.

b.

c.

d.

e.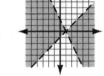

41. If $f(x) = 2x - 3$, $g(x) = x + \frac{3}{2}$, and $f\big(g(z)\big) = 6$, then $z =$

A. -3
B. -1
C. 0
D. 1
E. 3

42. $1 + \frac{2}{3} + \frac{4}{9} + \frac{8}{27} + \cdots =$

A. 3
B. π
C. 3π
D. 9
E. ∞

43. Which of the following matrices is *not* invertible?

A. $\begin{bmatrix} 1 & 2 \\ 3 & 6 \end{bmatrix}$

B. $\begin{bmatrix} 1 & 2 \\ 3 & 0 \end{bmatrix}$

C. $\begin{bmatrix} 1 & 3 \\ 6 & 2 \end{bmatrix}$

D. $\begin{bmatrix} 1 & 2 \\ 6 & 3 \end{bmatrix}$

E. $\begin{bmatrix} 2 & 3 \\ 1 & 6 \end{bmatrix}$

44. A drawer contains eight pairs of socks. If Susan chooses four socks at random from the drawer, what are the chances that she will get two left socks and two right socks?

    A. 1/2
    B. 2/5
    C. 1/64
    D. 28/65
    E. 56/143

45. $\left(2 + \sqrt{3}\right) \div \left(2 - \sqrt{3}\right) =$

    A. 2
    B. $\sqrt{3}$
    C. 7
    D. $1 + 4\sqrt{3}$
    E. $7 + 4\sqrt{3}$

46. The half-life of the isotope ^{226}Ra is about 1,600 years. A certain sample of rock contains two grams of radioactive ^{226}Ra. How much did it contain 8,000 years ago?

    A. 0.4 g
    B. 5 g
    C. 10 g
    D. 20 g
    E. 64 g

47. Which of the following lines includes a diameter of the circle $(x-1)^2 + (y-2)^2 = 4$?

    A. $y = x - \frac{1}{2}$
    B. $y = 2x + 2$
    C. $y = 2x + 4$
    D. $y = 3x - 1$
    E. $y = 4x + 2$

48. Sylvia, who is just over five feet tall, stands 195 feet away from the base of a tower and looks toward the top of the tower with a 45°angle of inclination. Approximately how tall is the tower?

    A. 100 ft.
    B. 200 ft.
    C. 400 ft.
    D. $200\sqrt{3}$ ft.
    E. $400\sqrt{3}$ ft.

49. If $p^q = r$, then which of the following is equivalent to q?

    A. $p \ln r$
    B. $r \ln p$
    C. $\frac{\ln r}{\ln p}$
    D. $\frac{\ln p}{\ln r}$
    E. $\log_r p$

WRITTEN ESSAY

Some people feel that video games actually promote intelligence. They say that strategy games force players to make strategic choices, plan ahead, and react in appropriate ways to challenges. Others feel that video games are simply a mindless pastime, and that time would be better spent doing something constructive like reading or participating in sports. Write an essay to a parent who is deciding whether they should allow their child to play video games. Take a position on whether video games are a valuable activity or simply a waste of time. Use arguments and examples to support your position.

Answer Explanations

SENTENCE SKILLS

Sentence Correction

1. D: Answer choice A is incorrect because *severely* is an adverb and not an adjective. B and C are incorrect because *problem* instead of the grammatically correct *problems* is used. D uses the correct, plural form *problems* and uses adjectives to describe the problems.

2. A: The sentence implies that *velocity* is used to indicate more than one value, which eliminates B and D. The phrase refers to velocity, which is singular, but the construction of choice C would correctly refer to a plural noun. Choice A agrees with the singular, noun and the *and* indicates that velocity is used to indicate more than one value.

3. B: Answer choice B uses the grammatically correct *their* instead of *there*. The *to* indicates the companies are using these sites for something, and *services* and *products* agree with each other because they are both plural.

4. C: Answer choice C states that an autoclave is a tool used *to sterilize*. A and B, which begin with *to sterilizing* and *for sterilize*, are not grammatically correct. D indicates that the machine is used to sterilize a single tool and needle, which does not make sense in the context of the sentence.

5. D: Answer choices A and C are incorrect because they imply that the bizarre creatures are something other than electric eels. The *a* in choice B does not agree with the plural *electric eels*. Choice D is best because it is grammatically correct and identifies electric eels as the bizarre creatures being discussed in the sentence.

6. A: Answer choice B is incorrect because the plural *key factors* and the singular *is* do not agree. The *taking* in choice C makes it incorrect. Choice D has a misplaced comma. Choice A makes sense and the singular *a key factor* and *is* agree with each other.

7. C: Choice C is the only choice that has correctly placed commas. The *numerous moons* and the *Great Red Spot* both refer to the planet Jupiter, which is maintained in answer choice C.

8. A: Answer choice B is incorrect because of the misplaced apostrophe. C has two unnecessary commas. Answer choice D is too wordy, and *landfills wastes* sounds quite awkward. Answer choice A is succinct, the comma is in the correct place, and it expresses the information is a clear way that is not awkward.

9. D: Answer choices A and C are incorrect because *large* is used in front of *attributable* and *attributed.* Both of these phrases are grammatically incorrect. B describes *the growing of the securities industry*, which is quite awkward. D is the best choice because it refers to *the growth of the security industry* and uses the phrase *largely attributed*, which is grammatically correct.

10. C: The correct way to refer to a person, in this case Monet, is through the use of the pronoun *whose*, which eliminates A and D. Two paintings are identified, so the plural form must be used, eliminating choice B. Choice C uses *whose* and *paintings*, indicating there is more than one, making it the correct choice.

22

Construction Shift

11. B: The original sentence indicates that bats and dolphins are able to do many things, including locating food sources like insects or fish through a process known as echolocation. Answer choice B best expresses the fact that locating food is accomplished through echolocation. Answer choice C cannot logically follow the phrase. Answer choices A and D do not tell how bats and dolphins locate food.

12. A: The new sentence begins with the phrase "even though," indicating that a contrast is being constructed. "Even though carbon dating is not always entirely accurate, it is still an accepted method" provides this contrast, while the other choices do not.

13. D: Melting water, chopped wood, and ripped paper are identified in the original sentence as examples of physical changes that are easy to distinguish from chemical changes. Therefore, answer choices A and C are entirely incorrect. Answer choice B indicates that these objects are easy to recognize, but the sentence should convey that they are examples of physical changes that are easy to recognize, making this choice somewhat inaccurate. Choice D is best because it identifies the previously mentioned objects as examples of physical changes.

14. D: The only phrase that describes something developed by Sigmund Freud is D. Answer choice A does not identify what the *it* is referring to, and B cannot logically follow the given phrase. Answer choice C describes ways to access repressed memories, but these were not developed by Freud.

15. C: A focus on nature and ascribing importance to everyday occurrences are identified in the original sentence as important characteristics of Romantic poetry. Answer choice C clearly identifies them as characteristics, and is the only choice that can logically follow the given phrase.

16. A: The Sugar Act is identified in the first sentence as something that was implemented in 1764 by England. Therefore, answer choice A is the best choice. Answer choice B does not indicate what was implemented. Answer choice C indicates where but not what was implemented, and D does not tell the reader what was implemented.

17. B: The phrase "even though" indicates a contrast. Answer choice A is more of an agreement than a contrast. Answer choice C is somewhat redundant, and D cannot logically follow the given phrase. Answer choice B provides a contrast because the given phrase talks about spills in water, while choice B talks about spills on land. It is also a logical choice because "it" in choice B refers to "the phrase" that is mentioned in the given phrase.

18. C: C is the only choice that provides a distinction between then and now. The given phrase says that radar was *once* used to determine the presence of objects, and C indicates that radar can *now* determine other things as well.

19. A: The word "by" indicates a cause/effect relationship. By measuring whether people respond significantly more favorably when given a real drug, something is being accomplished. Answer choices C and D do not imply this relationship. Answer choice B does not make logical sense in the context of the sentence. Answer choice A states "the effectiveness of a drug," which is a good choice because it could logically be followed with a phrase like "can be determined."

20. D: The word "while" is used to establish a contrast, making D the obvious choice. The given phrase speaks about *some people*, while D identifies *other employees*, which creates an effective contrast.

23

READING COMPREHENSION

1. B: Answer choices A and C are mentioned only briefly. D is discussed, but it falls under the more general purpose of the passage, which is discussing why the Amazon Rainforest is a valuable area that should be protected.

2. C: Answer choice A is not a logical conclusion because there is no indication that Gardner ranked the intelligences in any way. Answer choice B cannot be concluded from the passage, as there is no mention of the value placed on intrapersonal intelligences in a traditional academic environment. IQ tests are not mentioned at all, so we cannot conclude anything about them based on this passage. Answer choice C is the correct choice. Those with interpersonal intelligence interact well with others, so it is reasonable to assume they would perform well in a group setting.

3. C: Answer choices A and B are touched upon only very briefly. Answer choice D is discussed, but it is encompassed by the broader purpose of the passage, which is to outline the most important considerations related to passwords.

4. B: Answer choice B is the most logical conclusion. The passage states that, "Primary sources are the more direct type of information. They are accounts of an event that are produced by individuals who were actually present." Therefore, it is reasonable to assume that an account prepared by someone who was present would be more accurate than one prepared by somebody decades later who had to rely on the accounts of others.

5. A: Answer choices B and C are mentioned only briefly, and D is not really discussed in the passage. The passage focuses mainly on discussing some of the major benefits of sleep, so that is the main purpose of the passage.

6. B: Answer choice B is the logical conclusion. The passage states that "The king controlled all of the land in his jurisdiction. He divided this among a few barons. The barons then divided up the land they were given and distributed it to knights." If the barons divided up their lands, it would stand to reason that each baron would distribute his land to several knights. Therefore, there would have to be more knights than barons.

7. A: Answer choice B is not correct, because wild birds are not discussed at length. Answer choice C is not really discussed, and D is touched upon only briefly. The passage focuses on lack of preening and excessive preening, which are both examples of abnormal preening behavior. The main purpose of the passage is to discuss abnormal preening in birds.

8. D: The passage states that "Animals that are herbivores will find the winters extremely tough, because all of the vegetation will have died off by the time winter arrives. Hibernation is essentially a way of dealing with this food shortage." Therefore, D is the correct answer. Answer choice A is the purpose of migration, and answer choices B and C are not mentioned.

9. B: Answer choices A, C, and D are all mentioned in the passage, but they are part of the overall purpose, which is to give an overview of how leeches have been used throughout history.

10. C: The passage states that "Obviously, this was bad news for music artists and record labels because they weren't making any profits from downloaded music." Therefore, answer choice C is the correct choice. None of the other choices are identified as problems associated with file-sharing sites.

11. A: The first sentence states that the only purpose of zoos is to allow greedy people to profit. The second sentence challenges the first, however, pointing out that a key purpose of zoos is to protect endangered animals.

12. B: The first sentence states that elephants are capable of human-like behaviors. The second sentence states that elephants bury their dead and visit graves, which provides examples of human-like behaviors.

13. D: The first sentence mentions that cardiovascular health is a benefit of aerobic exercise. The second sentence mentions low resting heart rates and fewer cardiovascular problems, which are signs of good cardiovascular health. Therefore, the second sentence expands on the information in the first.

14. C: The first sentence identifies a problem: persisting high rates of teen pregnancy in spite of advancements in contraceptive technology. The second sentence offers a possible explanation: young people aren't being informed about how they can access contraceptives.

15. D: The first sentence mentions that various solutions for solving a Rubik's cube exist. The second sentence explains one in greater detail. Therefore, the second sentence expands on the information in the first.

16. A: The first sentence states that many people use digital devices to keep track of their schedules. The second describes several key advantages of PDAs that could possibly explain their popularity. Therefore, the sentences provide a statement and an explanation.

17. B: The first sentence states that DDT is a substance believed to be harmful to people and wildlife. The second sentence states that its use was banned in the United States. This ban is a direct result of the discovery of the harm that DDT can cause.

18. C: The two sentences express the same idea, and no new information is added in the second sentence. Therefore, the two sentences repeat the same information.

19. A: The first sentence states students should make decisions about what they will study in university based on their interests. The second states they should make decisions based on the job market. The second sentence directly contradicts the first.

20. B: The first sentence states that biological weapons have been used by militaries for many years. The second sentence tells about an army that threw poisonous snakes onto the ships of their enemies. The second sentence provides an example of biological weapons that were used long ago.

ARITHMETIC

1. B: To convert an improper fraction to a mixed number, divide the numerator by the denominator: the quotient is the integer part of the mixed number, and the remainder is the numerator. $27 \div 8 = 3$ with a remainder of 3, so $\frac{27}{8} = 3\frac{3}{8}$.

2. A: In order to subtract decimal numbers, write them one above the other with the decimal points aligned, filling in zeroes as necessary, and then carry out the subtraction normally, placing the decimal point in the same position in the result:

```
  6.32
- 3.50
  2.82
```

3. D: The volume of a right rectangular prism—that is, a box shape—is equal to the product of its length, width, and height. So the volume of the given box is equal to $(20 \text{ cm})(30 \text{ cm})(15 \text{ cm}) = 9,000 \text{ cm}^3$.

4. B: The number of people who voted for the proposition is 9.5% of 51,623. If we only require an approximation, we can round 9.5% to 10%, and 51,623 to 50,000. Then 9.5% of 51,623 is about 10% of 50,000, or $(0.1)(50,000) = 5,000$.

5. D: In mathematics, the word "of" indicates multiplication. So $\frac{5}{6}$ of $\frac{3}{4}$ is just $\frac{5}{6} \times \frac{3}{4} = \frac{5 \times 3}{6 \times 4} = \frac{15}{24}$, which reduces to $\frac{15 \div 3}{24 \div 3} = \frac{5}{8}$.

6. D: If there are three feet in a yard, then to convert yards to feet we just multiply by 3. So five yards is equal to $5 \times 3 = 15$ feet. Likewise, since there are twelve inches in a foot, to convert feet to inches, we just multiply by 12. So 15 feet is equal to $15 \times 12 = 180$ inches.

7. B: To multiply decimals, first multiply the numbers normally ignoring the decimal point; then, position the decimal point in the answer so that the number of digits after the decimal point in the product is equal to the *sum* of the number of digits after the decimal point in both factors. Performing the multiplication without regard to the decimal point first, we get $22 \times 313 = 6886$. Since there is one digit after the decimal point in 2.2 and one digit after the decimal point in 31.3, there should be two digits after the decimal point in the product, which is therefore 68.86.

8. D: To find the average of a set of numbers, add the numbers together and divide by how many there are (in this case, three). So, to find the average of $\frac{1}{3}$, $\frac{2}{3}$, and $\frac{1}{4}$, we first add them together. To add fractions, we can convert them all to fractions which have the least common denominator, which is in this case 12: $\frac{1}{3} + \frac{2}{3} + \frac{1}{4} = \frac{1 \times 4}{3 \times 4} + \frac{2 \times 4}{3 \times 4} + \frac{1 \times 3}{4 \times 3} = \frac{4}{12} + \frac{8}{12} + \frac{3}{12} = \frac{4+8+3}{12} = \frac{15}{12}$, which reduces to $\frac{15 \div 3}{12 \div 3} = \frac{5}{4}$. To get the average, we now divide this sum by three: $\frac{5}{4} \div 3 = \frac{5}{4} \times \frac{1}{3} = \frac{5 \times 1}{4 \times 3} = \frac{5}{12}$.

9. A: To convert a number to scientific notation, move the decimal point until there is just one digit before it (not counting leading zeroes), and rewrite the number as the result times a power of ten. The exponent of the power of ten is equal to the number of places the decimal point was moved—positive if the decimal was moved left, and negative if the decimal was moved right. Starting with 0.0023, to put only one digit before the decimal point, we have to move the decimal point three places to the right. Therefore, $0.0023 = 2.3 \times 10^{-3}$.

10. B: Since all students who answered her survey said they prefer one of the three flavors, the percentages must add up to 100%. Therefore, the percentage of students who prefer strawberry must be $100\% - (35\% + 40\%) = 100\% - 75\% = 25\%$.

11. C: To find out how much more milk he needs, subtract the amount he has from the amount he needs: $2\frac{1}{4} - 1\frac{1}{2}$. To add or subtract mixed numbers, first convert them to improper fractions. We

26

can do this by multiplying the integer part by the denominator and adding that to the numerator. So, $2\frac{1}{4} = \frac{2\times4+1}{4} = \frac{9}{4}$, and $1\frac{1}{2} = \frac{1\times2+1}{2} = \frac{3}{2}$. Now convert both fractions so that they share the lowest common denominator, which in this case is 4. $\frac{9}{4}$ already has a denominator of 4, so we need to convert $\frac{3}{2}$: $\frac{3}{2} = \frac{3\times2}{2\times2} = \frac{6}{4}$. We can now subtract: $\frac{9}{4} - \frac{6}{4} = \frac{3}{4}$.

12. B: 15,012 is close to 15,000, and 19,938 is close to 20,000. We would therefore expect $\frac{15,012}{19,938}$ to be close to $\frac{15,000}{20,000} = \frac{15}{20} = \frac{15\div5}{20\div5} = \frac{3}{4}$.

13. A: To multiply a fraction by a decimal, it is helpful to either convert both numbers to decimals or both to fractions. If we convert $\frac{2}{5}$ to a fraction, we divide 2 by 5, putting a decimal point after the 2 and keeping track of where the digits of the quotient are relative to the decimal point:

$$
\begin{array}{r}
.4 \\
5\overline{)2.0} \\
\underline{2\,0} \\
0
\end{array}
$$

So $\frac{2}{5} = 0.4$, and $\frac{2}{5} \times 2.5 = 0.4 \times 2.5$. $4 \times 25 = 100$, and since 0.4 and 2.5 each have one digit after the decimal point, the product should have two digits after the decimal point, so the answer is 1.00, or simply 1.

Alternately, if we convert 2.5 to a fraction, we can write $2.5 = 2 + 0.5 = 2 + \frac{5}{10} = 2 + \frac{1}{2} = \frac{5}{2}$. Then, $\frac{2}{5} \times \frac{5}{2} = \frac{2\times5}{5\times2} = \frac{10}{10} = 1$.

14. A: To find Sam's average speed, we have to divide the total distance he travelled by the total travel time. Note that fifteen minutes is a quarter hour, and forty-five minutes is $\frac{3}{4}$ hours. During the first fifteen minutes, therefore, the distance Sam runs is 8 mph $\times \frac{1}{4}$ hour = 2 miles. During the next forty-five minutes, he jogs 4 mph $\times \frac{3}{4}$ hours = 3 miles. So, the total distance he runs is $2 + 3 = 5$ miles. The time he runs is $\frac{1}{4}$ hour $+ \frac{3}{4}$ hours = 1 hour, so his average speed is 5 miles / 1 hour = 5 miles per hour.

15. D: Since the five angles together go all the way around the central point, they must add up to a complete rotation of 360°. Therefore, if the angles are all equal, each angle must have a measure of $\frac{360°}{5} = 72°$.

16. B: Translate "What percent of 800 is 40?" into the mathematical equation $x\% \cdot 800 = 40$. To solve, divide 40 by 800 and convert the answer to a percent. To divide a smaller number by a larger, add a decimal point after the smaller number and add zeroes as necessary, putting the decimal point in the same position in the quotient as it appears in the dividend:

$$\begin{array}{r} .05 \\ 800\overline{)40.00} \\ \underline{40\ 00} \\ 0 \end{array}$$

So $40 \div 800 = 0.05$. To express this as a percent, just multiply by 100, which moves the decimal point two places to the left: $0.05 = 5\%$.

17. C: To convert a fraction into a decimal, divide the numerator by the denominator. To divide a smaller number by a larger, add a decimal point after the smaller number and add zeroes as necessary, putting the decimal point in the same position in the quotient as it appears in the dividend:

$$\begin{array}{r} 0.1875 \\ 16\overline{)3.0000} \\ \underline{1\ 6} \\ 1\ 40 \\ \underline{1\ 28} \\ 120 \\ \underline{112} \\ 80 \\ \underline{80} \\ 0 \end{array}$$

ELEMENTARY ALGEBRA

18. D: To simplify the inequality $3 - 2x < 5$, we can first subtract 3 from both sides: $3 - 2x - 3 < 5 - 3 \Rightarrow -2x < 2$. Now, we can divide both sides of the inequality by -2. When an inequality is multiplied or divided by a negative number, its direction changes ($<$ becomes $>$, $\leq$ becomes $\geq$, and vice versa). So $-2x < 2$ becomes $\frac{-2x}{-2} > \frac{2}{-2}$, or $x > -1$.

19. C: $6\left(-\frac{2}{3}\right) - 2\left(-\frac{7}{2}\right) = \left(\frac{6}{1}\right)\left(-\frac{2}{3}\right) - \left(\frac{2}{1}\right)\left(-\frac{7}{2}\right) = -\left(\frac{6}{1}\right)\left(\frac{2}{3}\right) - \left(-\left(\frac{2}{1}\right)\left(\frac{7}{2}\right)\right) = -\frac{6\times2}{1\times3} + \frac{2\times7}{1\times2} = -\frac{12}{3} + \frac{14}{2} = -4 + 7 = 3$.

20. C: The nth root of x is equivalent to x to the power of $\frac{1}{n}$, i.e. $\sqrt[n]{x} = x^{\frac{1}{n}}$. This means in particular that $\sqrt[3]{x} = x^{\frac{1}{3}}$, and so $\left(\sqrt[3]{(x^4)}\right)^5 = \left((x^4)^{\frac{1}{3}}\right)^5$. Raising a power to another power is equivalent to multiplying the exponents together, so this equals $x^{4\times\frac{1}{3}\times5} = x^{\frac{20}{3}}$.

21. B: $\left(\frac{x^2-5x+6}{x+1}\right) \times \left(\frac{x+1}{x-2}\right) = \frac{(x^2-5x+6)\times(x+1)}{(x+1)\times(x-2)}$. Before carrying out the multiplication of the polynomials, notice that there is a factor of $x + 1$ in both the numerator and denominator, so the expression reduces to $\frac{x^2-5x+6}{x-2}$. We can simplify further by factoring the numerator. One way to factor a quadratic expression with a leading coefficient of 1 is to look for two numbers that add to

28

the coefficient of x (in this case -5) and multiply to the constant term (in this case 6). Two such numbers are -2 and -3: $(-2) + (-3) = -5$ and $(-2) \times (-3) = 6$. So $x^2 - 5x + 6 = (x-2)(x-3)$. That means $\frac{x^2-5x+6}{x-2} = \frac{(x-2)(x-3)}{x-2}$. The $x - 2$ in the numerator and denominator can cancel, so we are left with just $x - 3$. (Note that if $x = -1$ or $x = 2$, the obtained simplified expression would not be true: either value of x would result in a denominator of zero in the original expression, so the whole expression would be undefined. Therefore, it is necessary to state that these values of x are excluded from the domain. For a domain of $x > 2$, both -1 and 2 are excluded as possible values of x.)

22. A: When $x \geq 0$, $|x| = x$, so it is not true that $|x| > x$. However, when < 0, $|x| = -x$. This means x is negative and $|x|$ is positive, and since any positive number is greater than any negative number, $|x| > x$ when $x < 0$.

23. C: A method commonly taught to multiply two binomials is the "FOIL" method, an acronym for First, Outer, Inner, Last: multiply the first terms of each factor, then the outer terms, and so forth. Applied to $(\sqrt{2} + \sqrt{3}) \times (2 + \sqrt{6})$, this yields $(\sqrt{2})(2) + (\sqrt{2})(\sqrt{6}) + (\sqrt{3})(2) + (\sqrt{3})(\sqrt{6}) = 2\sqrt{2} + \sqrt{12} + 2\sqrt{3} + \sqrt{18}$. Two of these terms can be simplified: $12 = 4 \times 3$, so $\sqrt{12} = \sqrt{4} \times \sqrt{3} = 2\sqrt{3}$, and $18 = 9 \times 2$, so $\sqrt{18} = \sqrt{9} \times \sqrt{2} = 3\sqrt{2}$. Therefore, the produce can be written as $2\sqrt{2} + 2\sqrt{3} + 2\sqrt{3} + 3\sqrt{2}$, which simplifies to $5\sqrt{2} + 4\sqrt{3}$ after like terms are combined.

24. C: The area of the square base is just the square of the side length: $(700 \text{ ft})^2 = 490{,}000 \text{ ft}^2$. Since we only need an approximation, we can round that to $500{,}000 \text{ ft}^2$, or half a million square feet. The volume is therefore $\frac{1}{3}Bh \approx \frac{1}{3}\left(\frac{1}{2} \text{ million ft}^2\right)(450 \text{ ft}) = \frac{450}{6} \text{ million ft}^3 = 75 \text{ million ft}^3$.

25. A: To evaluate $\frac{x^3+2x}{x+3}$ at $= -1$, substitute in -1 for x in the expression: $\frac{(-1)^3+2(-1)}{(-1)+3} = \frac{(-1)+(-2)}{2} = \frac{-3}{2} = -\frac{3}{2}$.

26. C: If the exam has 30 questions, and the student answered C questions correctly and left B questions blank, then the number of questions the student answered incorrectly must be $30 - B - C$. He gets one point for each correct question, or $1 \times C = C$ points, and loses $\frac{1}{2}$ point for each incorrect question, or $\frac{1}{2}(30 - B - C)$ points. Therefore, one way to express his total score is $C - \frac{1}{2}(30 - B - C)$

27. C: $|-2| = |2| = 2$, $|3| = 3$, and $|-1| = 1$. So $\frac{|2|+|-2|}{|3|-|-1|} = \frac{2+2}{3-1} = \frac{4}{2} = 2$.

28. D: To add the two fractions, first rewrite them with the least common denominator, which is in this case y^3. $\frac{x}{y^3}$ already has this denominator, and we can rewrite $\frac{x^2}{y^2}$ as $\frac{x^2 \times y}{y^2 \times y} = \frac{x^2 y}{y^3}$. Thus, $\frac{x^2}{y^2} + \frac{x}{y^3} = \frac{x^2 y}{y^3} + \frac{x}{y^3} = \frac{x^2 y+x}{y^3}$.

29. B: Call the number of people present at the meeting x. If each person hands out a card to every *other* person (that is, every person besides himself), then each person hands out $x - 1$ cards. The total number of cards handed out is therefore $(x - 1)$. Since we are told there are a total of 30 cards handed out, we have the equation $(x - 1) = 30$, which we can rewrite as the quadratic equation $x^2 - x - 30 = 0$. We can solve this equation by factoring the quadratic expression. One way to do this is to find two numbers that add to the coefficient of x (in this case -1) and that multiply to the constant term (in this case -30). Those two numbers are 5 and -6. Our factored equation is therefore $(x + 5)(x - 6) = 0$. To make the equation true, one or both of the factors must be zero: either $+5 = 0$, in which case $x = -5$, or $x - 6 = 0$, in which case $x = 6$. Obviously, the number of people at the meeting cannot be negative, so the second solution, $x = 6$, must be correct.

COLLEGE-LEVEL MATHEMATICS

30. B: The area of the parallelogram can be determined in several ways. Recall that the area of a parallelogram is equal to the magnitude of the cross product of the vectors representing two adjacent sides. We can express the side connecting the points $(0, 0)$ and $(4, 5)$ as the vector $(4 - 0, 5 - 0) = (4,5)$ and the side connecting the points $(0, 0)$ and $(6, 2)$ as the vector $(6 - 0, 2 - 0) = (6, 2)$. For two vectors in the xy plane (u_1, v_1) and (u_2, v_2), the magnitude of the cross product is $|u_1 v_2 - u_2 v_1|$, which in this case would be $|4 \times 2 - 6 \times 5| = |-22| = 22$.

31. D: To solve the equation $3^x = 2$, we need to take the logarithm base three of both sides of the equation. (b^x and $\log_b x$ are inverse functions and cancel each other out for any positive base b.) Then we have $\log_3(3^x) = \log_3 2$, or simply $x = \log_3 2$. Alternatively, just keep in mind that $a^b = c$ is equivalent to $\log_a c = b$ for any positive a and c, so $3^x = 2$ is equivalent to $\log_3 2 = x$.

32. B: In general, any equation of the form $Ax^2 + Bxy + Cy^2 + Dx + Ey + F = 0$ describes a (possibly degenerate) conic section. (In the given equation, the constant term is on the right-hand side of the equation, but that's unimportant; we can easily convert it to the above form by simply subtracting 13 from both sides.) To determine which kind of conic section the equation corresponds to, we can look at the discriminant, $B^2 - 4AC$. If the discriminant is positive, the equation represents a hyperbola, if the discriminant is negative, the equation represents an ellipse or circle; and if the discriminant is zero, the equation represents a parabola. Here the discriminant is $6^2 - 4(9)(1) = 36 - 36 = 0$, so the equation represents a parabola.

33. E: One way to find an inverse function is to take the original equation describing the function, replace $f(x)$ with x and x with $f^{-1}(x)$, and then solve for $f^{-1}(x)$. In this case, $f(x) = \tan(2x + 4)$ becomes $x = \tan(2f^{-1}(x) + 4)$. To solve for $f^{-1}(x)$, first take the inverse tangent of both sides: $\tan^{-1} x = \tan^{-1}(\tan(2f^{-1}(x) + 4)) = 2f^{-1}(x) + 4$. Now subtract four from both sides: $\tan^{-1} x - 4 = 2f^{-1}(x)$. Finally, divide both sides by 2: $\frac{1}{2}(\tan^{-1} x - 4) = f^{-1}(x)$, or $f^{-1}(x) = \frac{1}{2}\tan^{-1} x - 2$.

34. D: $\sqrt[n]{x}$ is equivalent to $x^{\frac{1}{n}}$, so $\sqrt[5]{\left(\sqrt[8]{9^{10}}\right)^6}$ can be rewritten as $\left(\left((9^{10})^{\frac{1}{8}}\right)^6\right)^{\frac{1}{5}}$. When raising a power to another power, the exponents multiply, so this is equivalent to $9^{10 \times \frac{1}{8} \times 6 \times \frac{1}{5}}$. $10 \times \frac{1}{8} \times 6 \times \frac{1}{5} = \frac{10}{1} \times \frac{1}{8} \times \frac{6}{1} \times \frac{1}{5} = \frac{10 \times 1 \times 6 \times 1}{5 \times 1 \times 8 \times 1} = \frac{60}{40}$, which reduces to $\frac{3}{2}$. The original expression therefore reduces to $9^{\frac{3}{2}}$, which is equal to $\left(\sqrt{9}\right)^3 = 3^3 = 27$.

35. B: The absolute value of a complex number $a + bi$ is equal to $\sqrt{a^2 + b^2}$. $|6 + 2i|$ is therefore $\sqrt{6^2 + 2^2} = \sqrt{36 + 4} = \sqrt{40} = \sqrt{4} \times \sqrt{10} = 2\sqrt{10}$.

36. C: The volume of a rectangular solid is the product of its length, width, and height, $= l \times w \times h$. In this case, we're told the room is twice as wide as it is tall, and three times as long as it is wide, so we can write $w = 2h$ — or, equivalently, $h = \frac{w}{2}$ —and $l = 3w$. Our volume equation then becomes $V = 3w \times w \times \frac{w}{2} = \frac{3}{2}w^3$. Setting that equal to the given volume of 12,000 ft³, we have

$\frac{3}{2}w^3 = 12,000$, so $w^3 = \frac{2}{3} \times 12,000 = 8,000$, and $w = \sqrt[3]{8,000} = 20$ ft.

37. D: A power of a binomial can be expanded by the binomial theorem, $(x + y)^n = \sum_{i=0}^{n} \binom{n}{i} x^{n-i}y^i$, where $\binom{n}{i}$ is the binomial coefficient, which can be derived either from Pascal's triangle or from the equation $\binom{n}{i} = \frac{n!}{i!(n-i)!}$. That is, $(x + y)^n = \binom{n}{0}x^n + \binom{n}{1}x^{n-1}y + \binom{n}{2}x^{n-2}y^2 + \cdots + \binom{n}{n}y^n$. In this case, where $n = 5$, $x = a$, and $y = 2b$, we have:

$$(a + 2b)^5 = \binom{5}{0}a^5 + \binom{5}{1}a^4(2b) + \binom{5}{2}a^3(2b)^2 + \binom{5}{3}a^2(2b)^3 + \binom{5}{4}a(2b)^4 + \binom{5}{5}(2b)^5$$
$$= (1)a^5 + (5)a^4(2b) + (10)a^3(4b^2) + (10)a^2(8b^3) + (5)a(16b^4) + (1)(32b^5)$$
$$= a^5 + 10a^4b + 40\,a^3b^2 + 80\,a^2b^3 + 80ab^4 + 32b^5$$

The only one of the answer choices that does not appear as a term of this polynomial is D, $40ab^4$.

38. C: The sum of two logarithms of the same base is equal to the logarithm of the product, and the difference of two logarithms of the same base is equal to the logarithm of the quotient. That is, $\log_b x + \log_b y = \log_b(xy)$, and $\log_b x - \log_b y = \log_b \frac{x}{y}$. Therefore, $\ln 7 + \ln 5 - \ln 3 = \ln(7 \times 5) - \ln 3 = \ln 35 - \ln 3 = \ln \frac{35}{3}$.

39. A: $\sec\theta = \frac{1}{\cos\theta}$, or, equivalently, $\cos\theta = \frac{1}{\sec\theta}$. Therefore, if $\sec\theta = 2$, then $\cos\theta = \frac{1}{2}$. $\cos\theta = \frac{1}{2}$ when $\theta = 60°$ or $300°$; $\sin 60° = \frac{\sqrt{3}}{2}$ and $\sin 300° = -\frac{\sqrt{3}}{2}$. Alternatively, use the Pythagorean identity $\sin^2\theta + \cos^2\theta = 1$ to find $\sin\theta$, so $\sin^2\theta = 1 - \cos^2\theta$, and $\sin\theta = \pm\sqrt{1 - \cos^2\theta} = \pm\sqrt{1 - \left(\frac{1}{2}\right)^2} = \pm\sqrt{1 - \frac{1}{4}} = \pm\sqrt{\frac{3}{4}} = \pm\frac{\sqrt{3}}{2}$. (Whether the sine is positive or negative depends on what quadrant the angle is in; there is not enough information given in the problem to determine that, which is why the problem only asks which of the answer choices is a *possible* value for $\sin\theta$.)

40. C: The five choices all have the two lines that mark the boundaries of the inequalities plotted identically; the only difference is which sides are shaded. It's therefore not necessary to check that the lines are correct; simply determine which of the areas bounded by the lines pertain to the system of inequalities. One way to do that is to pick a point in each region and check whether it satisfies the inequalities. For instance, in the region on the left, we can pick the origin, $(0, 0)$. Since $0 - 0 \not> 1$ and $2(0) + 0 \not> 2$, this does not satisfy either inequality. From the top region we can choose, for example, the point $(0, 3)$. $0 - 3 \not> 1$, so this fails to satisfy the first inequality. From the bottom region we can choose, for instance, $(0, -2)$. $0 - (-2) > 1$, so the first inequality is satisfied, but $2(0) + (-2) \not> 2$, so the second is not. Finally, from the rightmost region we can choose, for example, the point $(2, 0)$. $2 - 0 > 1$ and $2(2) + 0 > 2$, so both inequalities are satisfied; this is the only region that should be shaded in.

41. E: $f\big(g(x)\big) = f\left(x + \frac{3}{2}\right) = 2\left(x + \frac{3}{2}\right) - 3 = 2x + 2 \times \frac{3}{2} - 3 = 2x + 3 - 3 = 2x$. So the statement that $f\big(g(z)\big) = 6$ is equivalent to $2z = 6$. Dividing both sides of this equation by 2, we find $z = 3$.

42. A: The numbers $1, \frac{2}{3}, \frac{4}{9}, \frac{8}{27}, \ldots$ form a geometric sequence, since the ratio of any two consecutive terms is the same, namely $\frac{2}{3}$. What the problem is asking for, then, is the sum of an infinite geometric sequence. This sum exists (and is finite) whenever the absolute value of the common ratio r is less than one; since $\left|\frac{2}{3}\right| < 1$, that condition is satisfied. The formula for the sum of an infinite geometric series is $S_\infty = \frac{a_1}{1-r}$, where a_1 is the first term of the series and r is the common ratio; putting in the appropriate values of $a_1 = 1$ and $r = \frac{2}{3}$, we get $S_\infty = \frac{1}{1-\frac{2}{3}} = \frac{1}{\frac{1}{3}} = 3$.

43. A: A square matrix A is invertible—that is, there exists another matrix A^{-1} such that $A\,A^{-1} = A^{-1}A = I$, where I is the identity matrix, $\begin{bmatrix} 1 & 0 \\ 0 & 1 \end{bmatrix}$ (or its higher-order version)—if and only if its *determinant* is nonzero. For a 2×2 matrix $\begin{bmatrix} a & b \\ c & d \end{bmatrix}$ like the ones given in the answer choices, the determinant is $ad - bc$. The determinant of the matrix in choice A is $1 \times 6 - 2 \times 3 = 6 - 6 = 0$, so that matrix is not invertible. The determinants of the matrices in the other four choices are -6, -16, -9, and 9, respectively: since these determinants are all nonzero, the four matrices in choices B, C, D, and E are all invertible.

44. D: To determine the probability of Susan's drawing two left and two right socks from the drawer, we can determine the total number of possible sets of two left socks and two right socks, and divide by the total number of possible sets of four socks. If there are eight pairs of socks in the drawer, then there are eight left socks, so the total number of possible sets of two left socks that can be drawn is $_8C_2 = \binom{8}{2} = \frac{8!}{2!(8-2)!} = \frac{8 \times 7 \times 6!}{2! \times 6!} = \frac{56}{2} = 28$. By the same logic, there are also 28 possible sets of two right socks that can be drawn. Since there are 16 socks in the drawer in all, the total number of possible sets of four socks that can be drawn is $_{16}C_4 = \binom{16}{4} = \frac{16!}{4!(16-4)!} = \frac{16 \times 15 \times 14 \times 13 \times 12!}{4! \times 12!} = \frac{16 \times 15 \times 14 \times 13}{4 \times 3 \times 2 \times 1}$

$= 4 \times 5 \times 7 \times 13 = 1820$. The probability of her drawing two left socks and two right socks is therefore $\frac{28 \times 28}{1820} = \frac{28}{65}$.

45. E: We can write the quotient as a fraction: $\frac{2+\sqrt{3}}{2-\sqrt{3}}$. Now, we need to *rationalize the denominator* -- that is, to convert this fraction to a form without any radicals in the denominator. To do this, we multiply both sides of the fraction by the conjugate of the denominator: $\frac{(2+\sqrt{3}) \times (2+\sqrt{3})}{(2-\sqrt{3}) \times (2+\sqrt{3})}$. We can simplify both the numerator and the denominator by using the FOIL method, for First, Inner, Outer, Last:

$\left(2 + \sqrt{3}\right) \times \left(2 + \sqrt{3}\right) = 2 \times 2 + 2 \times \sqrt{3} + \sqrt{3} \times 2 + \sqrt{3} \times \sqrt{3} = 4 + 2\sqrt{3} + 2\sqrt{3} + 3 = 7 + 4\sqrt{3}$

$\left(2 - \sqrt{3}\right) \times \left(2 + \sqrt{3}\right) = 2 \times 2 + 2 \times \sqrt{3} + \left(-\sqrt{3}\right) \times 2 + \left(-\sqrt{3}\right) \times \sqrt{3} = 4 + 2\sqrt{3} - 2\sqrt{3} - 3 = 1$

The fraction then becomes $\frac{7+4\sqrt{3}}{1}$, or simply $7 + 4\sqrt{3}$.

46. E: The half-life of an isotope is the amount of time it takes for it to decay to half its former amount. 8,000 years is five times the half-life of 1,600 years, so the amount of ^{226}Ra would have been halved five times. That is, the original amount would have been multiplied by $\left(\frac{1}{2}\right)^5 = \frac{1}{32}$. So if we call the original amount of ^{226}Ra x, then we know $\frac{1}{32}x = 2$ g, so $x = 2$ g $\times$ 32 $= 64$ g.

47. D: Any diameter of a circle must pass through its center, and, conversely, any line through the center of a circle includes a diameter of the circle. The question, then, is equivalent to asking which of the given lines passes through the center of the circle. The standard form of the equation of a circle is $(x - h)^2 + (y - k)^2 = r^2$, where r is the circle's radius and (h, k) is its center. In the case of the given equation, $(x - 1)^2 + (y - 2)^2 = 4$, $h = 1$ and $k = 2$, so the center of the circle is the point $(1, 2)$. The simplest way to check which line passes through the point $(1, 2)$ is just to substitute $x = 1$ and $y = 2$ into the equation of each line and see which equation remains true. Since $2 \neq 1 - \frac{1}{2}$, $2 \neq 2 \times 1 + 2$, $2 \neq 2 \times 1 + 4$, and $2 \neq 4 \times 1 + 2$, the lines in choices A, B, C, and E do not pass through the point $(1, 2)$. However, $2 = 3 \times 1 - 1$, so the equation of line D is satisfied.

48. B: From the given information, we can sketch the following figure (not to scale):

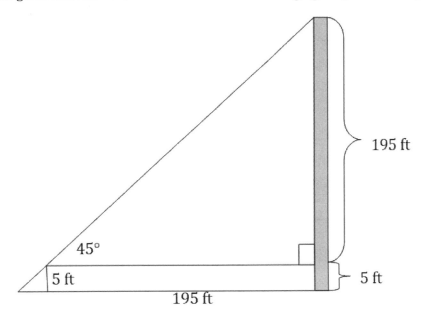

The legs of a 45°-45°-90° triangle are congruent; therefore, the vertical distance from the top of the tower to Sylvia's horizontal line of sight is the same as the distance Sylvia stands from the tower, 195 feet. Since Sylvia is approximately 5 feet tall, the height of the tower is approximately 195 ft + 5 ft $= 200$ ft.

49. C:. By the relation of logarithms to exponents, if $p^q = r$ then $q = \log_p r$. This, however, is not one of the answer choices. (Choice E is $\log_r p$, but this reverses the p and the r and is not the same thing.) However, we can use the change of base formula, $\log_x y = \frac{\log_b y}{\log_b x}$ for any positive base b. In particular, we can choose $b = e$, the base of the natural logarithm, so $\log_p r = \frac{\log_e r}{\log_e p} = \frac{\ln r}{\ln p}$.

Practice Test #2

SENTENCE SKILLS

Sentence Correction

Directions for questions 1–10

Select the best version of the underlined part of the sentence. The first choice is the same as the original sentence. If you think the original sentence is best, choose the first answer.

1. If he stops to consider the ramifications of this decision, it is probable that he will rethink his original decision a while longer.

    A. it is probable that he will rethink his original decision.
    B. he will rethink his original decision over again.
    C. he probably will rethink his original decision.
    D. he will most likely rethink his original decision for a bit.

2. When you get <u>older," she said "you will no doubt</u> understand what I mean."

    A. older," she said "you will no doubt
    B. older" she said "you will no doubt
    C. older," she said, "you will no doubt
    D. older," she said "you will not

3. Dr. Anderson strolled past the nurses, examining a bottle of pills.

    A. Dr. Anderson strolled past the nurses, examining a bottle of pills.
    B. Dr. Anderson strolled past the nurses examining a bottle of pills.
    C. Examining a bottle of pills Dr. Anderson strolled past the nurses.
    D. Examining a bottle of pills, Dr. Anderson strolled past the nurses.

4. Karl and Henry raced to the reservoir, climbed the ladder, and then they dove into the cool water.

    A. raced to the reservoir, climbed the ladder, and then they dove into
    B. first raced to the reservoir, climbed the ladder, and then they dove into
    C. raced to the reservoir, they climbed the ladder, and then they dove into
    D. raced to the reservoir, climbed the ladder, and dove into

5. Did either Tracy or Vanessa realize that her decision would be so momentous?

    A. Tracy or Vanessa realize that her decision would be
    B. Tracy or Vanessa realize that each of their decision was
    C. Tracy or Vanessa realize that her or her decision would be
    D. Tracy or Vanessa realize that their decision would be

6. Despite their lucky escape, Jason and his brother could not hardly enjoy themselves.

    A. Jason and his brother could not hardly enjoy themselves.
    B. Jason and his brother could not enjoy themselves.
    C. Jason and Jason's brother could not hardly enjoy themselves.
    D. Jason and his brother could not enjoy them.

7. Stew recipes call for rosemary, parsley, thyme, and these sort of herbs.

    A. for rosemary, parsley, thyme, and these sort of herbs.
    B. for: rosemary; parsley; thyme; and these sort of herbs.
    C. for rosemary, parsley, thyme, and these sorts of herbs.
    D. for rosemary, parsley, thyme, and this sorts of herbs.

8. Mr. King, an individual of considerable influence, created a personal fortune and gave back to the community.

    A. an individual of considerable influence, created a personal fortune and gave back
    B. an individual of considerable influence, he created a personal fortune and gave back
    C. an individual of considerable influence created a personal fortune and gave back
    D. an individual of considerable influence, created a personal fortune and gave it back

9. She is the person whose opinion matters the most.

    A. She is the person whose opinion matters the most.
    B. She is the person to whom opinion matters the most.
    C. She is the person who matters the most, in my opinion.
    D. She is the person for whom opinion matters the most.

10. Minerals are nutritionally significant elements <u>that assist to make your body</u> work properly.

    A. that assist to make your body
    B. that help your body
    C. that making your body
    D. that work to make your body

Construction Shift

Directions for questions 11–20

Rewrite the sentence in your head following the directions given below. Keep in mind that your new sentence should be well written and should have essentially the same meaning as the original sentence.

11. The Burmese python is a large species of snake that is native to parts of southern Asia, although the snake has recently begun infesting the Florida Everglades and causing environmental concerns by devouring endangered species.

Rewrite the sentence, beginning with the phrase,

    The Burmese python has recently caused environmental concerns in the Florida Everglades.

The words that follow will be:

    A. because it is devouring endangered species in Florida
    B. where it has made a home for itself away from its origins in southern Asia
    C. by leaving its native home of southern Asia with an infestation of its natural prey
    D. and is altering the delicate balance of species in that area

12. In the wild, the Burmese python typically grows to around twelve feet in length, but in captivity the snakes can often grow much longer than that, to upwards of fifteen or twenty feet in length.

Rewrite the sentence, beginning with the phrase,

Burmese pythons in captivity can grow to be as long as fifteen or twenty feet.

The words that follow will be:

    A. as a result of the controlled environment that allows them to eat more
    B. while it is typically shorter in the wild
    C. but in the wild are shorter and may only be twelve feet long
    D. which is much longer than a python in the wild grows to be

13. Florida biologists and environmentalists blame the exotic animals industry for the snake's introduction into the Everglades, because many snake owners are unable or unwilling to continue taking care of the creature once it grows too large and becomes too expensive.

Rewrite the sentence, beginning with the phrase,

The Burmese python can grow large and become too expensive for snake owners to maintain.

The words that follow will be:

    A. and Florida biologists and environmentalists blame the exotic animals industry
    B. so the python has been introduced into the Everglades
    C. leaving the exotic animals industry at risk in the United States
    D. resulting in abandoned snakes that have infested the Everglades

14. Lawmakers called for action against owning Burmese pythons after a pet python got out of its cage in a Florida home and killed a young child while she was sleeping, a situation that left responsible snake owners objecting and claiming that this was an isolated event.

Rewrite the sentence, beginning with the phrase,

Responsible Burmese python owners have claimed that the death of a young child in Florida after a python attack was an isolated event.

The words that follow will be:

    A. but lawmakers have called for action against owning the pythons
    B. because the python accidentally got out of its cage and attacked the child
    C. that does not reflect accurately on conscientious snake owners
    D. resulting in angry lawmakers who called for a prohibition of Burmese pythons

15. Biologists were initially concerned that the Burmese python could spread throughout much of the United States, due to its ability to adapt to its environment, but recent evidence suggests that the snake is content to remain within the Everglades.

Rewrite the sentence, beginning with the phrase,

Recent evidence suggests that the Burmese python is content to remain within the Everglades.

The words that follow will be:

    A. due to its ability to adapt to its environment
    B. and comes as a surprise to biologists who believed the snake would spread outside Florida
    C. despite concerns that the snake could spread throughout much of the United States
    D. because it is unable to adapt to cooler environments outside of south Florida

16. The most prolific predator in the Florida Everglades has always been the alligator, which preys on local birds and wildlife, while the introduction of the Burmese python adds another, and often insatiable, predator to compete with the alligator.

Rewrite the sentence, beginning with the phrase,

> *The introduction of the Burmese python to the Everglades adds another predator to compete with the alligator.*

The words that follow will be:

A. which has always been the most prolific predator in the Everglades
B. thus leaving the local birds and wildlife in serious danger of becoming endangered
C. and the alligator was never as serious a predator as the python has become
D. which does not have the python's reputation for being insatiable

17. Not only does the Burmese python compete with the alligator for prey, but it also competes with the alligator as prey, because pythons have been known to engorge full-grown alligators, thus placing the python at the top of the food chain and leaving them with no native predators in the Everglades.

Rewrite the sentence, beginning with the phrase,

> *The Burmese python is now at the top of the food chain in the Everglades and has no native predator.*

The words that follow will be:

A. so it competes with the alligator as prey
B. as evidence shows that pythons are capable of engorging full-grown alligators
C. although the python still competes with alligators for prey
D. leaving the Everglades with a serious imbalance of predators

18. Biologists and environmentalists recognize the considerable dangers of the python's expansion in the Everglades as it consumes endangered creatures native to that area, and in one instance researchers were shocked to discover that the tracking device for a tagged rodent led them to the python who had already consumed the unlucky creature.

Rewrite the sentence, beginning with the phrase,

> *Researchers in the Everglades were shocked to discover that the tracking device for a tagged rodent led them to the python who had already consumed the unlucky creature.*

The words that follow will be:

A. thus showing how the python is destroying endangered species within the Everglades
B. causing concerns that the python expansion might be more dangerous than biologists and environmentalists originally believed
C. which was one of the few of its species that had managed to survive the python expansion in the Everglades
D. leaving biologists and environmentalists to recognize the considerable dangers of the python's expansion in the Everglades

19. In an attempt at controlling the python, Florida dispatched hunters to destroy as many pythons as possible, but after several months of searching the hunters were only able to make a dent in the python population of thousands by killing several dozen.

Rewrite the sentence, beginning with the phrase,

> *The python population of thousands was reduced only by several dozen.*

The words that follow will be:

A. even after many months of searching for and destroying the creatures

B. because the hunters were only given a few months for the task and needed more time to destroy as many pythons as possible

C. after the hunters sent to destroy as many pythons as possible failed to make a dent in the number

D. resulting in concerns that more hunters were needed to locate and destroy as many pythons as possible

20. Although eradication is preferred when non-native species are introduced into the United States, researchers have found that is it virtually impossible, and controlling the species becomes the only real option in avoiding the destruction of native habitats and endangered species.

Rewrite the sentence, beginning with the phrase,

> *Controlling an invasive species is the only real option in avoiding the destruction of native habitats and endangered species.*

The words that follow will be:

A. because the total eradication of non-native species that are introduced into the United States is virtually impossible

B. because the total eradication of non-native species that are introduced into the United States is generally frowned upon

C. although researchers prefer the total eradication of non-native species and continue to make efforts to destroy the python in the Everglades

D. in spite of the many attempts at totally eradicating the non-native species that are introduced into the United States

READING COMPREHENSION

Directions for questions 1–10

Read the statement or passage and then choose the best answer to the question. Answer the question based on what is stated or implied in the statement or passage.

1. The so-called anti-aging industry is worth a staggering amount of money in North America. Women are sold all sorts of creams and ointments, and are promised that these will make them look younger over time. Unfortunately, these claims are entirely false. Lotions cannot penetrate to the inner layers of the skin where wrinkles typically form. Therefore, no over-the-counter creams are effective at erasing lines and wrinkles.

According to the author, the anti-aging industry

    A. targets its products at men and women equally.
    B. sells products that are highly effective.
    C. is still a relatively small industry.
    D. sells goods that do not do what they promise.

2. There is a clear formula that many students are taught when it comes to writing essays. The first is to develop an introduction, which outlines what will be discussed in the work. It also includes the thesis statement. Next comes the supporting paragraphs. Each paragraph contains a topic sentence, supporting evidence, and finally a type of mini-conclusion that restates the point of the paragraph. Finally, the conclusion sums up the purpose of the paper and emphasizes that the thesis statement was proven.

After the topic sentence,

    A. a thesis statement is included.
    B. supporting evidence is presented.
    C. the conclusion is stated.
    D. the author outlines what will be discussed.

3. The importance of a comfortable work space cannot be overstated. Developing a comfortable work environment is relatively simple for employers. Ergonomic chairs, large computer screens, personal desk space, and some level of privacy are all essential. This involves some expense, but not a great deal. Not surprisingly, employees are happier in this type of environment, but it is the employers who really benefit. Reduced sick time, higher levels of employee satisfaction, higher productivity, and more creativity have all been observed.

The main idea expressed in this passage is

    A. a comfortable work space is not as important as people say.
    B. developing a comfortable work space is easy.
    C. establishing a comfortable work space is not expensive.
    D. employers benefit greatly when they provide comfortable work spaces.

4. Planning weddings is tough. One important part of the planning process is choosing bridesmaid dresses. Although there used to be a lot of rules when it came to picking out a color, many of them are not observed any more. However, one that is still observed is that the bridesmaids should not wear the same color as the bride. The most popular colors for bridesmaid dresses in recent years have been white and black.

It can be concluded that

    A. picking dresses is the hardest part of planning a wedding.
    B. many brides are choosing to wear colors other than white.
    C. most bridesmaids are allowed to choose their own dress.
    D. bridesmaids were not traditionally allowed to wear black.

5. Those so-called green fuels may not be as environmentally friendly as once thought. For example, producing natural gas is a much more labor intensive process than producing an equal amount of conventional gasoline. Also, producing natural gas involves burning fossil fuels. Transporting natural gas also involves burning fossil fuels.

The weakness of green fuels is that

    A. they are not as abundant as conventional fuel.
    B. they require a lot more work to produce.
    C. burning them releases fossil fuels.
    D. they must be transported greater distances.

6. The media has done a lot to promote racism in North America. For example, it was found that the majority of crimes discussed on the nightly news featured African American suspects. However, when the total number of crimes committed in North American was examined, it was found that white people were also suspects 50% of the time.

If the above information were true, it could be concluded that

    A. there are more white criminals than African American criminals.
    B. most people believe that African Americans commit more crimes.
    C. many crimes committed by white people are not discussed on the news.
    D. the total number of crimes committed has decreased in the last several years.

7. Many people feel that the use of stem cells in research is unethical. However, they fail to realize that such research could lead to cures for some of the world's most troubling diseases. Diseases like Parkinson's and MS could possibly be cured through the use of stem cells, and those with spinal cord injuries could possibly walk again. Therefore, it is entirely ethical to engage in stem cell research aimed at easing the suffering of those who have life-altering conditions.

The main purpose of the passage is

    A. to discuss why people believe stem cell research is unethical.
    B. to discuss the possible benefits of stem cell research.
    C. to identify diseases that have been cured through stem cell research.
    D. to argue that not conducting stem cell research is unethical.

8. Many people do not know the difference between precision and accuracy. While accuracy means that something is correct, precision simply means that you are able to duplicate results and that they are consistent. For example, if there was a glass of liquid that was 100 degrees, an accurate measurement would be one that was close to this temperature. However, if you measured the temperature five times, and came up with a measurement of exactly 50 degrees each time, your measurement would be extremely precise, but not accurate.

The term accurate results refers to

    A. results that are correct.
    B. results that are consistent.
    C. results that can be duplicated.
    D. results that are measurable.

9. Literacy rates are lower today than they were fifteen years ago. Then, most people learned to read through the use of phonics. Today, whole language programs are favored by many educators.

If these statements are true, it can be concluded that

    A. whole language is more effective at teaching people to read than phonics.
    B. phonics is more effective at teaching people to read than whole language.
    C. literacy rates will probably continue to decline over the next 15 years.
    D. the definition of what it means to be literate is much stricter now.

10. George Washington was a remarkable man. He was born in 1732. Shortly before becoming the President of the United States in 1789, Washington was an important leader in the American Revolutionary War from 1775 to 1783. After retiring, he returned to Mount Vernon in 1797. A short time later, John Adams made him commander in chief of the United States Army again. This was done in anticipation that the country might go to war with France.

Almost immediately after serving as a leader in the American Revolutionary War

    A. Washington returned to Mount Vernon.
    B. Washington was made commander in chief of the U.S. Army.
    C. Washington became the President of the United States.
    D. Washington decided to go into retirement.

11. The history of the samurai in Japan is believed to date back to the late 7th century during a period of administrative reform that greatly reorganized Japan. In 663, Japan lost the Battle of Hakusukinoe against the Tang Dynasty of China.

What does the second sentence do?

    A. It undermines the first.
    B. It explains the first.
    C. It restates the first.
    D. It refutes the first.

12. The reform process did not initially create the warrior system that later became the samurai. The bureaucrats known as samurai were administrative officials whose name came from a word that meant "to serve."

What does the second sentence do?

>   A. It examines the first.
>   B. It reaffirms the first.
>   C. It clarifies the first.
>   D. It defines a term.

13. During attempts to conquer the island of Honshu, the 8ᵗʰ- and 9ᵗʰ-century Emperor Kammu relied on his serf army to accomplish the task. The emperor used clan members from his aristocracy to succeed in adding Honshu to Japan.

What does the second sentence do?

>   A. It explains the first.
>   B. It undermines the first.
>   C. It offers essential evidence.
>   D. It classifies the main idea.

14. The aristocratic clan members represented a powerful force in Emperor Kammu's army, due to their horseback skills and knowledge of weaponry, and he dismissed them following the victory at Honshu. Kammu slowly lost power in the 9ᵗʰ century.

What does the second sentence do?

>   A. It presents a new theory.
>   B. It transitions to a new idea.
>   C. It adds crucial information.
>   D. It implies a consequence.

15. The aristocratic clans began establishing their social and political power within Japanese culture. The clan members made powerful marriages, created treaties with other clans, and placed themselves under the code of the Bushido.

What does the second sentence do?

>   A. It offers a comparison.
>   B. It classifies a system.
>   C. It elaborates on an idea.
>   D. It refutes the main idea.

16. The Bushido represents an ethical system that shaped the clan leaders into a warrior class, or the samurai. The code of the Bushido encouraged personal honor, the responsibility of the warrior to the lord, and loyalty to the lord even to the point of death.

What does the second sentence do?

>   A. It develops the first.
>   B. It establishes an effect.
>   C. It contrasts with the first.
>   D. It establishes the main idea.

17. The samurai grew in political and social authority during the late 12th century and the early 13th century. In 1185, the samurai were successful during their participation in the Battle of Dan-no-Ura.

What does the second sentence do?

A. It examines the first.
B. It questions the main idea.
C. It offers comparative detail.
D. It suggests a cause.

18. By the end of the 13th century, the samurai grew to be more powerful than the aristocrats they were intended to support. The samurai loyalty to the lord, as required by the Bushido code, became a purely nominal fidelity.

What does the second sentence do?

A. It undermines the main idea.
B. It restates the point of the first.
C. It counters the presented theory.
D. It examines a supporting thought.

19. Eventually, the samurai were so successful that their warrior services were no longer as necessary as they had been in the past. The samurai began to turn to more artistic pursuits, such as writing poetry and composing music.

What does the second sentence do?

A. It provides comparative detail.
B. It establishes an argument.
C. It elaborates on the main idea.
D. It offers essential information.

20. Despite a commitment to honorable death, many samurai still feared the prospect of dying by violent means. The principles of Zen Buddhism that were practiced among the samurai included personal discipline, meditation, and self-realization.

What does the second sentence do?

A. It calls supporting information into question.
B. It elaborates on a theory presented in the first.
C. It suggests a cause and effect relationship.
D. It compares and contrasts two systems of thought.

ARITHMETIC

Solve the following problems and select your answer from the choices given. You may use the paper you have been given for scratch paper.

1. $4\frac{1}{5} - 2\frac{1}{3} =$

   A. $1\frac{13}{15}$
   B. $2\frac{1}{4}$
   C. $2\frac{2}{15}$
   D. $4\frac{1}{2}$

2. $\left(2.2 \times 10^3\right) \times \left(3.5 \times 10^{-2}\right) =$

   A. 7.7×10^{-6}
   B. 7.7×10^1
   C. 7.7×10^5
   D. 7.7×10^6

3. In the diagram to the right (not to scale), $x = 91°$ and $y = 42°$. What is z?

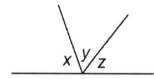

   A. $47°$
   B. $49°$
   C. $66\frac{1}{2}°$
   D. $133°$

4. Doug drives without backtracking from his apartment to a campsite in another state. After two hours, he is halfway to his destination. After four hours, he is two-thirds of the way there. Which of the following could represent the fraction of his travel distance he has covered after three hours?

   A. $\frac{2}{5}$
   B. $\frac{3}{5}$
   C. $\frac{3}{4}$
   D. $\frac{4}{5}$

5. What is 10% of 40%?

   A. 4%
   B. 30%
   C. 50%
   D. 400%

6. $2.62 \times 7.1 =$

   A. 1.462
   B. 14.62
   C. 16.062
   D. 18.602

7. Alan has a large number of cubical building blocks 4 cm on a side. He wants to use them to make a larger solid cube 20 cm on a side. How many building blocks will he need for this?

   A. 25
   B. 94
   C. 125
   D. 150

8. Which of the following is closest to $\frac{149}{1502}$?

   A. 0.012
   B. 0.77
   C. 0.103
   D. 0.151

9. Water drains from a bathtub at a rate of one gallon every fifteen seconds. If the bathtub initially has twelve gallons of water in it, how long will it take to drain completely?

   A. 48 seconds
   B. 1 minute 15 seconds
   C. 3 minutes
   D. 4 minutes

10. $\frac{7}{8} \times \frac{2}{3} \times \frac{4}{5} \times \frac{3}{7} =$

   A. $\frac{1}{7}$
   B. $\frac{1}{5}$
   C. $\frac{3}{8}$
   D. 1

11. What is the average of 2.02, 0.275, and 1.98?

   A. 1.1375
   B. 1.375
   C. 1.425
   D. 2.25

12. What is 60% of $\frac{5}{6}$?

   A. $\frac{1}{2}$
   B. $\frac{3}{4}$
   C. $\frac{5}{12}$
   D. $\frac{25}{36}$

13. A particular map has a scale of 1 inch = 5 miles. On the map, Lost Canyon Road is one foot long. How long is the actual road?

    A. 2.4 miles
    B. 6 miles
    C. 24 miles
    D. 60 miles

14. $3\frac{1}{4} + 2\frac{5}{6} =$

    A. $5\frac{1}{2}$
    B. $5\frac{3}{5}$
    C. $6\frac{1}{12}$
    D. $6\frac{1}{2}$

15. 50 is what percent of 40?

    A. 80
    B. 90
    C. 120
    D. 125

16. Which of the following is largest?

    A. 0.55
    B. 0.500
    C. 0.505
    D. 0.0555

17. All of the following represent the same number EXCEPT

    A. 0.05
    B. $\frac{1}{50}$
    C. 5×10^{-2}
    D. 5%

ELEMENTARY ALGEBRA

Solve the following problems and select your answer from the choices given. You may use the paper you have been given for scratch paper.

18. What is the value of $\frac{2x-2}{x+3}$ when $x = -1$?

    A. 0
    B. 1
    C. 2
    D. −2

19. Which of the following correctly represents the solution to the inequality $x^2 + 2x \geq x + 6$?

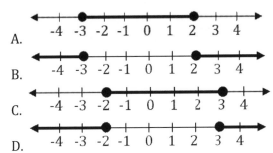

    A.
    B.
    C.
    D.

20. If $\frac{1}{2x} + \frac{1}{x} = \frac{1}{6}$, then $x =$

    A. 2
    B. 4
    C. 9
    D. 12

21. A building has a number of floors of equal height, as well as a thirty-foot spire above them all. If the height of each floor in feet is h, and there are n floors in the building, which of the following represents the building's total height in feet?

    A. $n + h + 30$
    B. $nh + 30$
    C. $30n + h$
    D. $30h + n$

22. $x(y - 2) + y(3 - x) =$

    A. $xy + y$
    B. $-2x + 3y$
    C. $2xy - 2x + 3y$
    D. $xy + 3y - x - 2$

23. Which of the following lists of numbers is ordered from least to greatest?

    A. $1, \frac{1}{3}, -\frac{1}{4}, \frac{1}{5}$
    B. $\frac{1}{5}, -\frac{1}{4}, \frac{1}{3}, 1$
    C. $-\frac{1}{4}, 1, \frac{1}{3}, \frac{1}{5}$
    D. $-\frac{1}{4}, \frac{1}{5}, \frac{1}{3}, 1$

24. In the figure to the right, the height of the triangle is three times the height of the square. If the square's width is s, what is the total area of the figure?

   A. $\frac{5}{2}s^2$

   B. $4s^2$

   C. $s^2 + \frac{3}{2}s$

   D. $s^2 + 3s$

25. $(x+6)(x-6) =$

   A. $x^2 - 12x - 36$

   B. $x^2 + 12x - 36$

   C. $x^2 + 12x + 36$

   D. $x^2 - 36$

26. If $x + 2y = 3$ and $-x - 3y = 4$, then $x =$

   A. 1

   B. 5

   C. 7

   D. 17

27. At a school carnival, three students spend an average of $10. Six other students spend an average of $4. What is the average amount of money spent by all nine students?

   A. $5

   B. $6

   C. $7

   D. $8

28. $-\frac{3}{2}\left(\frac{1}{2} + \frac{1}{3}\right) - \frac{2}{3}\left(\frac{1}{2} - \frac{3}{4}\right) =$

   A. $-1\frac{5}{12}$

   B. $-1\frac{1}{12}$

   C. $-1\frac{1}{2}$

   D. $1\frac{5}{12}$

29. How many solutions are there to the equation $\left|x^2 - 2\right| = x$?

   A. 0

   B. 1

   C. 2

   D. 4

COLLEGE-LEVEL MATH

Solve the following problems and select your answer from the choices given. You may use the paper you have been given for scratch paper.

30. If $\sqrt{2}^2 \cdot 2^{\sqrt{2}} = \left(\sqrt{2}^{\sqrt{2}}\right)^x$, then $x =$

    A. 2
    B. $\sqrt{2}$
    C. $2\sqrt{2}$
    D. $2^{\sqrt{2}}$
    E. $2 + \sqrt{2}$

31. **The interior of what shape is described by the following two inequalities?**
$$x^2 + y^2 < 4$$
$$x + y > 3$$

    A. A circle
    B. A semicircle
    C. A circular segment smaller than a semicircle
    D. A circular segment larger than a semicircle
    E. None; this system of inequalities has no solution.

32. $\dfrac{\ln 81}{\ln 3} =$

    A. 3
    B. $3\sqrt{3}$
    C. 4
    D. $\ln 3$
    E. $\ln 27$

33. **Which of the following is a root of $x^2 - 4x + 5$?**

    A. 4
    B. $10i$
    C. $1 - i$
    D. $2 + i$
    E. $4 - i$

34. **In the triangle to the right, which of the following is equal to $\sin \theta$?**

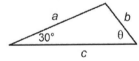

    A. $\dfrac{a}{2b}$
    B. $\dfrac{2b}{a}$
    C. $\dfrac{a}{2c}$
    D. $\dfrac{2a}{c}$
    E. $\dfrac{b}{ac}$

49

35. If the lines $y = ax + b$ and $y = bx + 2a$ intersect at the point $(2, 3)$, then $a =$

A. 0

B. $\frac{2}{3}$

C. 1

D. $\frac{3}{2}$

E. 3

36. What is the product of three consecutive odd integers, if the one in the middle is x?

A. $x^2 - 3x$

B. $x^2 - 5x$

C. $x^3 - x$

D. $x^3 - 4x$

E. $x^3 + x - 4$

37. $f(x) = ax^b + cx + d$, where a, b, c, and d are all integers. The equation $f(x) = 0$ has exactly one solution, which does *not* occur at a maximum or minimum of $f(x)$. Which of the following *must* be true?

A. a is positive.

B. a is negative.

C. b is odd.

D. b is even.

E. c is zero.

38. Six people sit around a circular table at a party. If two of these people are the party's hosts and must sit next to each other, how many different possibilities are there for the order of the six people around the table? (Rotations are not counted as different orders.)

A. 24

B. 48

C. 120

D. 240

E. 288

39. Which of the following graphs corresponds to the equation $y = 2 \sin(\pi x - \pi)$?

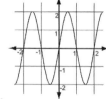
A.

B.
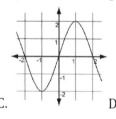
C.
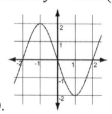
D.
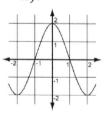
E.

40. If $f(x) = e^{2x}$ and f^{-1} is the inverse of f, then $f\left(f^{-1}(f(x))\right) =$

A. e^{2x}

B. $e^{2 \ln x}$

C. $e^{2x} \ln x$

D. $\ln\left(\frac{1}{2} e^{2x}\right)$

E. $e^{2 \ln\left(\frac{1}{2} e^{2x}\right)}$

41. What geometric shape is defined by the equation $ax + by + cz + d = 0$, where $a, b, c, d \neq 0$?

    A. A point
    B. A line
    C. A plane
    D. A sphere
    E. A hyperboloid

42. $\dfrac{x^7 + 2x^6 + x^5}{x^4 - x^2} =$

    A. $x^3 + 2z$
    B. $x^3 + x + 1$
    C. $\dfrac{x^5 + x^3}{x^2}$
    D. $\dfrac{x^4 + x^3}{x - 1}$
    E. $\dfrac{x^5 + x^3}{x^2 - 1}$

43. A chest is filled with large gold and silver coins, weighing a total of thirty pounds. If each gold coin weighs 12 ounces, each silver coin weighs 8 ounces, and there are fifty coins in all, how many gold coins does the chest contain? (There are sixteen ounces in a pound.)

    A. 10
    B. 15
    C. 20
    D. 25
    E. 30

44. An ellipse is described by the equation $3x^2 + 4y^2 = 48$. What is the length of its major axis?

    A. $2\sqrt{3}$
    B. 4
    C. $4\sqrt{3}$
    D. 8
    E. 12

45. The first three terms of a geometric sequence are 80, 120, and 180. Which of the following is equal to the tenth term of the sequence?

    A. $\dfrac{5 \times 3^9}{2^5}$
    B. $\dfrac{5 \times 3^{10}}{2^7}$
    C. $\dfrac{5 \times 2^4}{3^{10}}$
    D. $\dfrac{5 \times 2^{13}}{3^9}$
    E. $\dfrac{5 \times 2^{14}}{3^{10}}$

46. If $f(x) = e^{x-3}$, $g(x) = 2x - 1$, and $h(x) = f(x) + g(x)$, then $h(3) =$
    A. 2
    B. 3
    C. 4
    D. 5
    E. 6

47. If $2 \sec \theta = \tan^2 \theta$, which of the following is a possible value for $\sec \theta$?
    A. 2
    B. $\sqrt{2}$
    C. $\sqrt{2} - 1$
    D. $2 - \sqrt{2}$
    E. $1 + \sqrt{2}$

48. The population of the town of Wrassleton has tripled every ten years since 1950. If P_0 is the town's population in 1950 and t is the number of years since 1950, which of the following describes the town's growth during this time?
    A. $P(t) = 10\, P_0^{3t}$
    B. $P(t) = P_0^{\frac{3}{10}t}$
    C. $P(t) = P_0 \times 3^{\frac{t}{10}}$
    D. $P(t) = P_0 \times \left(\frac{3}{10}\right)^t$
    E. $P(t) = \left(\frac{3}{10} P_0\right)^t$

49. If $f(1) = 2$, $g(2) = 3$, $f^{-1}(3) = 4$, and $g^{-1}(4) = 1$, which of the following is *not* necessarily true?
    A. $f\big(g(1)\big) = 3$
    B. $f\big(g(3)\big) = 1$
    C. $g\big(f^{-1}(2)\big) = 4$
    D. $g^{-1}\big(f^{-1}(3)\big) = 1$
    E. $g(2) = f(4)$

WRITTEN ESSAY

Prepare an essay of about 300-600 words on the topic below.

Merit pay for teachers is the practice of giving increased pay based upon the improvement in student performance. It is a controversial idea among educators and policy makers. Those who support this idea say that, with it, school districts are able to select and retain the best teachers and to improve student performance. Others argue that merit pay systems lead to teacher competition for the best students and to test-driven teaching practices that are detrimental to the overall quality of education.

In your essay, select either of these points of view, or suggest an alternative approach, and make a case for it. Use specific reasons and appropriate examples to support your position and to show how it is superior to the others.

Answer Explanations

SENTENCE SKILLS

Sentence Correction

1. C: The original sentence is redundant and wordy.

2. C: The syntax of the original sentence is fine, but a comma after *said* but before the open-quotation mark is required.

3. D: In the original sentence, the modifier is placed too far away from the word it modifies.

4. D: The verb structure should be consistent in a sentence with parallel structures.

5. A: The singular pronoun *her* is appropriate since the antecedents are joined by *or.* Also, the subjunctive verb form is required to indicate something indefinite.

6. B: The combination of *hardly* and *not* constitutes a double negative.

7. C: The plural demonstrative adjective *these* should be used with the plural noun *sorts.*

8. A: This sentence contains a number of parallel structures that must be treated consistently.

9. A: In this sentence, *whose* is the appropriate possessive pronoun to modify *opinion.*

10. B: Answer choice B is precise and clear. Answer choice A keeps the meaning, but is awkward and wordy. Answer choice C uses the wrong verb tense. Answer choice D would put the word *work* into the sentence twice. It is not completely incorrect, but it is not the best choice.

Construction Shift

11. A: Answer choice A best completes statement in the rewritten sentence by making the immediate connection between the environmental concerns and the reason for them. Answer choice B could work within the context of the sentence, but it does not create a sufficient link between the environmental concerns and their causes. Answer choice C provides information that is not contained within the original sentence, and answer choice D also adds information by noting that the "delicate balance" is altered. While this might be inferred from the original sentence, it cannot be added to the rewritten sentence.

12. C: Answer choice C accurately adds the statement of contrast about the python being shorter in the wild. Answer choice A adds information to the original sentence. Answer choice B is technically correct but does not contain as much information as answer choice C and is thus not the best choice. Answer choice D is also technically correct but does not provide the substance of the information that answer choice C contains.

13. D: Answer choice D creates the necessary link between the snake owners and the infestation of pythons in the Everglades. Answer choice A contains accurate information, but the sentence does not flow smoothly from one idea to the next. Answer choice B is true but is vague and fails to create a sufficient link between ideas. Answer choice C contains details that make no sense within the context of the sentence.

14. A: Answer choice A provides the sense of contrast that is contained within the original sentence by showing the differences between the responsible snake owners and the lawmakers. Answer choice B offers information that is contained within the original sentence but fails to provide a clear link between ideas. Answer choice C essentially repeats the information that is in the rewritten statement and is thus repetitive. Answer choice D, though correct, does not make a great deal of sense following up the information in the rewritten statement.

15. C: Answer choice C effectively restates the sentence by capturing the entire mood of the original. Answer choice A adds correct information, but it is incomplete with respect to the original idea. Answer choice B may be inferred to a degree, but there is not enough information in the original sentence to claim that the biologists were "surprised" about the results – only that they were "concerned" about the potential. Answer choice D adds information that is not within the original sentence.

16. A: Answer choice A correctly adds the necessary information about the alligator's traditional role within the Everglades. Answer choice B reassembles the information from the original sentence but does not provide the key detail about the alligator's place in the Everglades. Answer choices C and D add information that cannot be inferred from the original sentence.

17. B: Answer choice B provides the full information that is needed to complete the original idea. Answer choice A provides only partial information and is thus insufficient. Answer choice C is repetitive and does not offer any new information to complete the original idea. Answer choice D offers inferred information, but as this is not contained within the original sentence, it cannot be added.

18. D: Answer choice D adds the correct information about the concern that follows the python's expansion within the Everglades, without adding inferred information. Answer choice A is correct but is not necessarily effective in explaining the substance of the reason for concern. Answer choice B adds information that cannot be clearly inferred (i.e., what biologists and environmentalists originally believed about the python in the Everglades). Answer choice C adds information that has no place in the original sentence.

19. C: Answer choice C effectively links the ideas contained in the original sentence. Answer choice A is accurate but ineffective and incomplete, because it fails to explain *who* was doing the searching and destroying. Answer choices B and D add judgment statements that are not in the original sentence.

20. A: Answer choice A sufficiently links the ideas in the original sentence, connecting the reality of control with the hope for eradication. Answer choice B contradicts information that is not in the original sentence; that is to say, the original sentence states clearly that "eradication is preferred," not frowned upon. Answer choice C is partially correct but becomes incorrect with the added information about researchers continuing to search for means of eradication. Answer choice D contains correct information but does not encompass the full meaning of the original sentence and leaves out valuable information (i.e., the virtual impossibility of eradication).

READING COMPREHENSION

1. D: The passage states "Women are sold all sorts of creams and ointments, and are promised that these will make them look younger over time. Unfortunately, these claims are entirely false. Lotions cannot penetrate to the inner layers of the skin, which is where wrinkles form." Therefore, these goods do not deliver what they promise.

2. B: The topic sentence is placed at the beginning of each supporting paragraph. Supporting evidence is presented after the topic sentence in each supporting paragraph. The passage states "Next come the supporting paragraphs. Each paragraph contains a topic sentence, supporting evidence, and finally a type of mini-conclusion that restates the point of the paragraph."

3. D: The main idea discussed in the passage is that employers benefit the most from establishing a comfortable work space. The author points out that it is not extremely expensive, then identifies all of the benefits for employers: better productivity, less absenteeism, etc.

4. B: It can be concluded that many brides are choosing to wear colors other than white based on two statements in the passage. First, we know that bridesmaids do not wear the same color as the bride. Secondly, it is stated that white is a popular color for bridesmaid dresses. Therefore, since the color of the bridesmaid dress is not the same as the bride's dress, it can be concluded that the bride's dress is not white.

5. B: Many green fuels require more work to produce than conventional fuels. The passage states "producing natural gas is a much more labor-intensive process than producing an equal amount of conventional gasoline. Producing natural gas also involves burning fossil fuels."

6. C: This conclusion can be made based on two statements. First, the passage states that "the majority of crimes discussed on the nightly news featured African American suspects." Second, "it was found that white people were also suspects 50% of the time." Therefore, if half of all suspects are white, but the majority of suspects on the news are African American, it is reasonable to conclude that the news chooses not to report crimes that involve white suspects.

7. B: The main purpose of the passage is to discuss the possible benefits of stem cell research. The author states that many people feel it is unethical, but most of the passage is devoted to discussing the possible benefits of stem cell research. Cures for diseases and being able to repair spinal cord injuries are the possible benefits identified.

8. A: Accuracy is the same as correctness. The passage states "accuracy means that something is correct" and "if there was a glass of liquid that was 100 degrees, an accurate measurement would be one that was close to this temperature."

9. B: It can be concluded that phonics is a more effective way to learn to read for two reasons. First, the passage states that literacy rates are lower now than they were 15 years ago, meaning that more people knew how to read 15 years ago. Then, the passage states that phonics was the main way people learned how to read then. Therefore, based on these two facts, it can be concluded that phonics is more effective.

10. C: The passage states that "Shortly before becoming the President of the United States in 1789, Washington was an important leader in the American Revolutionary War from 1775 to 1783."

11. B: The second sentence explains the first by creating a link between the "period of administrative reform" and the failure at the Battle of Hakusukinoe. Answer choices A and D are incorrect, because the second sentence in no way undermines or refutes the first. Answer choice C is incorrect, because the second sentence does more than merely restate the first.

12. C: The second sentence clarifies the first by providing further detail about why the reform process in Japan "did not initially create the warrior system that later became the samurai." Answer choice A is incorrect, because it does not make sense in this context to say that the second sentence examines the first. Answer choice B is incorrect, because the second sentence does not just reaffirm

56

the first: it provides further detail to explain the main point. Answer choice D is incorrect, because it limits the purpose of the second sentence. While the second sentence does indeed define a term, that is not its role. The second sentence clarifies the meaning of the first; in the process of doing so, it also happens to define a term.

13. B: The second sentence creates a conflict with the first, because the first sentence notes that the Emperor Kammu had a "serf army," while the second mentions his army of "clan members from his aristocracy." Without the historical explanation that Kammu dismissed the original army to create the aristocratic army, the second sentence appears to undermine the first. Answer choice A is incorrect, because instead of explaining the first sentence, the second sentence raises questions. Answer choice C is incorrect, because the second sentence could be said to require essential evidence but does not provide it. Answer choice D is incorrect, because it makes no sense in the context of the two sentences.

14. D: The second sentence implies a consequence: that the Emperor Kammu's power declined as a result of his choice to dismiss his aristocratic army. Answer choice A is incorrect, because the second sentence suggests a cause-and-effect relationship with the first, but this is not the same as presenting a new theory. (And without the context of what defines a new theory, answer choice A makes little sense.) Answer choice B is incorrect, because the second sentence seems to suggest a conclusion rather than the start of something new. Answer choice C is incorrect, because no context for crucial information is created between the two sentences.

15. C: The second sentence builds on the first by explaining how the aristocratic clans established themselves in Japanese culture by making marriages, creating treaties, and placing themselves under the Bushido. Answer choice A is incorrect, because it makes no sense in the context of the two sentences – no comparison is presented or made here. Answer choice B is incorrect, because no system is really classified; rather, the developing social position of the aristocratic clans is explained. Answer choice D is incorrect, because the second sentence supports and explains the main idea instead of refuting it.

16. A: As in question 5, the second sentence develops the primary idea of the first sentence by providing more detail about the Bushido and its meaning for the samurai. Answer choice B is incorrect, because it makes no sense; the possible effect is examined in the first sentence not the second if the Bushido were to be viewed as a type of cause. Answer choice C is incorrect, because no contrast is created within these sentences. Answer choice D is incorrect, because it describes the role of the first sentence instead of the second.

17. D: In the first sentence, a possible effect is created: the samurai became powerful during the late 12th century and the early 13th century. The second sentence follows with a mention of their success in a late 12th century battle. Therefore, the second sentence suggests a possible cause for the development of power. Answer choice A is incorrect, because it makes no sense in the context of the two sentences. Answer choice B is incorrect, because the second sentence does not attempt to question any part of the first. Answer choice C is incorrect, because no comparative information is offered in the second sentence.

18. B: The second sentence essentially restates the point of the first, that the samurai became more powerful than their lords and that the loyalty was largely in name-only by the end of the 13th century. Answer choice A is incorrect, because instead of undermining the main idea, the second sentence reaffirms it. In the same way, answer choice C is incorrect, because the second sentence does not counter, but rather confirm. Answer choice D is incorrect, because the role of the second sentence is to reiterate and not to examine.

19. C: The second sentence elaborates on the main idea by providing more information about what the samurai did since they were no longer needed as warriors. Answer choice A is incorrect, because the second sentence is not so much comparing as it is explaining. Answer choice B is incorrect, because the argument is established in the first sentence; the second sentence merely supports the argument. Answer choice D is incorrect, because it is difficult to determine within the limited context that is provided whether or not the information in the second sentence is "essential." The main idea is presented in the first sentence and could stand on its own. The second sentence simply adds supporting detail.

20. C: The second sentence suggests a cause-and-effect relationship that cannot be obviously inferred from the first but that can still follow as a possible result. The first sentence notes that many samurai struggled with the idea of death, and the second sentence indicates that the samurai practiced Zen Buddhism – which offers the very teachings that warriors might use to handle the potential for violent death. Answer choice A is incorrect, because no supporting information is brought to bear. Answer choice B is incorrect, because the first sentence does not offer a theory; instead, it states a fact. Answer choice D is incorrect, because the two sentences have a cause-and-effect relationship but not a compare-and-contrast relationship.

ARITHMETIC

1. A: One way to add or subtract mixed numbers is to first convert them to improper fractions. We can do this by multiplying the integer part of the mixed number by the denominator and adding that product to the numerator; this sum is the numerator of the improper fraction, and its denominator is the same as the denominator in the fractional part of the mixed number. So $4\frac{1}{5} = \frac{4\times5+1}{5} = \frac{21}{5}$ and $2\frac{1}{3} = \frac{2\times3+1}{3} = \frac{7}{3}$. Convert each fraction so that they contain the lowest common denominator, which in this case is 15. $\frac{21}{5} = \frac{21\times3}{5\times3} = \frac{63}{15}$ and $\frac{7}{3} = \frac{7\times5}{3\times5} = \frac{35}{15}$. We can now subtract: $\frac{63}{15} - \frac{35}{15} = \frac{28}{15}$. Finally, we convert back to a mixed number by dividing the numerator by the denominator. The quotient is the integer part, and the remainder is the new numerator; the denominator remains the same. $28 \div 15 = 1$ with a remainder of 13, so $\frac{28}{15} = 1\frac{13}{15}$.

2. B: To multiply numbers in scientific notation, first multiply the significands (the part before the power of ten), then multiply the powers of ten; when multiplying two numbers with the same base, add the exponents and keeping that base. So, to multiply 2.2×10^3 and 3.5×10^{-2}, we first multiply 2.2 by 3.5. To multiply decimals, first multiply the numbers normally ignoring the decimal point; then, position the decimal point in the answer so that the number of digits after the decimal point in the product is equal to the *sum* of the number of digits after the decimal point in both factors. $22 \times 35 = 770$, and since there is one digit after the decimal point in 2.2 and one digit after the decimal point in 3.5, there should be two digits after the decimal point in the product, which therefore becomes 7.70, or 7.7. Now, multiply the powers of 10: $10^3 \times 10^{-2} = 10^{3+(-2)} = 10^1$. The final answer is 7.7×10^1.

3. A: Together, these three angles form a straight angle, or 180°. So, $x + y + z = 180°$, which means $z = 180° - x - y = 180° - 91° - 42° = 47°$.

4. B: If he has covered $\frac{1}{2}$ the distance after two hours, and $\frac{2}{3}$ the distance after four hours, and he does not backtrack, then the fraction of the distance he has covered after three hours must be between $\frac{1}{2}$ and $\frac{2}{3}$. To compare fractions, we can convert them to equivalent fractions with the least common denominator. The least common denominator of $\frac{2}{3}$ and $\frac{3}{4}$ is 12; $\frac{2}{3} = \frac{2\times4}{3\times4} = \frac{8}{12}$ and $\frac{3}{4} = \frac{3\times3}{4\times3} =$

$\frac{9}{12}$. Since $\frac{9}{12} > \frac{8}{12}$, $\frac{3}{4}$ is not between $\frac{1}{2}$ and $\frac{2}{3}$. The least common denominator of $\frac{1}{2}$ and $\frac{2}{5}$ is 10; $\frac{1}{2} = \frac{1 \times 5}{2 \times 5} = \frac{5}{10}$ and $\frac{2}{5} = \frac{2 \times 2}{5 \times 2} = \frac{4}{10}$. Since $\frac{4}{10} < \frac{5}{10}$, $\frac{2}{5}$ is not between $\frac{1}{2}$ and $\frac{2}{3}$. Similarly, $\frac{4}{5} = \frac{4 \times 4}{5 \times 4} = \frac{16}{20}$ and $\frac{3}{4} = \frac{3 \times 5}{4 \times 5} = \frac{15}{20}$; since $\frac{16}{20} > \frac{15}{20}$, $\frac{2}{5}$ is not between $\frac{1}{2}$ and $\frac{2}{3}$. However, $\frac{3}{5} = \frac{3 \times 2}{5 \times 2} = \frac{6}{10} = \frac{3 \times 4}{5 \times 4} = \frac{12}{20}$; $\frac{6}{10} > \frac{5}{10}$ and $\frac{12}{20} < \frac{15}{20}$, so $\frac{1}{2} < \frac{3}{5} < \frac{3}{4}$.

5. A: x percent is the same thing as $\frac{x}{100}$, and finding x percent of a number is the same as multiplying that number by x percent. This is true even when the number is itself a percent. So, 10% of 40% is $40\% \times 10\% = 40\% \times \frac{10}{100} = 40\% \times \frac{1}{10} = 4\%$.

6. D: To multiply decimals, first multiply the numbers normally ignoring the decimal point; then, position the decimal point in the answer so that the number of digits after the decimal point in the product is equal to the *sum* of the number of digits after the decimal point in both factors. $262 \times 71 = 18{,}602$; there are two digits after the decimal point in 2.62 and one digit after the decimal point in 7.1, so there should be three digits after the decimal point in the product, which is therefore 18.602.

7. C: The ratio of volumes on two objects of the same shape is equal to the *cube* of the ratio of their lengths. Therefore, if the ratio of the length of the large cube to that of a building block is $\frac{20 \text{ cm}}{4 \text{ cm}} = 5$, the ratio of the *volume* of the large cube to that of a building block is 5^3, or 125— so that is how many building blocks it will take to make the large cube.

8. C: 149 is close to 150, and 1502 is close to 1500. Therefore, we would expect $\frac{149}{1502}$ to be close to $\frac{150}{1500}$, which reduces to $\frac{1}{10}$. As a decimal, $\frac{1}{10} = 0.1$. Choice C is the closest to this number.

9. C: We can start by rewriting the rate of drainage in gallons per minute. $\frac{1 \text{ gallon}}{15 \text{ seconds}} \times \frac{60 \text{ seconds}}{1 \text{ minute}} = \frac{60 \text{ gallons}}{15 \text{ minutes}} = 4$ gallons/minute. This means that in t minutes, the tub will have drained $4t$ gallons. We are asked to find how long the tub will take to drain 12 gallons, so $4t = 12$; dividing both sides by 4, we find $t = 3$.

10. B: While we *could* multiply together all the numbers in the numerator and all the numbers in the denominator and then simplify, it would be easier to cancel what we can first. There is a factor of 7 in both the numerator and the denominator; we can cancel those. The same goes for a factor of 3. That leaves us with $\frac{1}{8} \times \frac{2}{1} \times \frac{4}{5} \times \frac{1}{1}$. We can go further, though; since $2 \times 4 = 8$, the 2 and the 4 in the numerator cancel the 8 in the denominator, leaving us with just $\frac{1}{1} \times \frac{1}{1} \times \frac{1}{5} \times \frac{1}{1}$, or simply $\frac{1}{5}$.

11. C: To find the average, add together all the numbers and then divide by how many there are (in this case three). In order to add decimal numbers, write them one above the other with the decimal points aligned and carry out the addition normally, placing the decimal point in the same position in the result:

```
  2.02
+ 0.275
+ 1.98
  4.275
```

Now, to divide, just carry out the division normally but put the decimal point in the same position in the quotient as ti appears in the dividend:

$$
\begin{array}{r}
1.425 \\
3\overline{)4.275} \\
\underline{3} \\
12 \\
\underline{12} \\
07 \\
\underline{6} \\
15 \\
\underline{15} \\
0
\end{array}
$$

12. A: When dealing with percentages or fractions, "of" generally means multiply; 60% of $\frac{5}{6}$ means $60\% \times \frac{5}{6}$. We can write $x\%$ as $\frac{x}{100}$; 60% is therefore $\frac{60}{100}$, which reduces to $\frac{6}{10} = \frac{3\times2}{5\times2} = \frac{3}{5}$. So 60% of $\frac{5}{6} = \frac{3}{5} \times \frac{5}{6} = \frac{3\times5}{5\times6} = \frac{3}{6} = \frac{1}{2}$.

13. D: One foot is equal to twelve inches, so the road is twelve inches long on the map. If the map's scale is 1 inch = 5 miles, then we can find the road's actual length by solving the proportion $\frac{12\text{ inches}}{x\text{ miles}} = \frac{1\text{ inch}}{5\text{ miles}}$, or simply $\frac{12}{x} = \frac{1}{5}$. One way to solve this is by cross-multiplying: $12 \times 5 = x \times 1$, so $x = 60$.

14. C: We can do this by multiplying the integer part of the mixed number by the denominator and adding that product to the numerator; this sum is the numerator of the improper fraction, and its denominator is the same as the denominator in the fractional part of the mixed number. So, $3\frac{1}{4} = \frac{3\times4+1}{4} = \frac{13}{4}$ and $2\frac{5}{6} = \frac{2\times6+5}{6} = \frac{17}{6}$. Convert each fraction to its equivalent so that both fractions contain the lowest common denominator, which in this case is 12. $\frac{13}{4} = \frac{13\times3}{4\times3} = \frac{39}{12}$ and $\frac{17}{6} = \frac{17\times2}{6\times2} = \frac{34}{12}$. We can now add: $\frac{39}{12} + \frac{34}{12} = \frac{73}{12}$. Finally, we convert back to a mixed number by dividing the numerator by the denominator. The quotient is the integer part, and the remainder is the new numerator; the denominator remains the same. $73 \div 12 = 6$ with a remainder of 1, so $\frac{73}{12} = 6\frac{1}{12}$.

15. D: Taking a percent of a number means multiplying by that percent: if 50 is $P\%$ of 40, then $50 = 40 \times P\%$. That means $P\%$ is just $\frac{50}{40}$. We can write that as a decimal by dividing, putting a decimal point after the dividend and adding zeroes as necessary:

$$
\begin{array}{r}
1.25 \\
40\overline{)50.00} \\
\underline{40} \\
10\,0 \\
\underline{8\,0} \\
2\,00 \\
\underline{2\,00} \\
0
\end{array}
$$

So $\frac{50}{40} = 1.25$. To convert to a percent, we can multiply by 100, which is equivalent to moving the decimal point two places to the right: $1.25 = 125\%$.

16. A: When comparing decimals, compare them one decimal place at a time. First compare the part before the decimal point; whichever has the largest whole part is largest. If the whole parts are equal, compare the tenths place, the place just after the decimal point; if they differ in that place, then whichever has the larger digit in that place is larger. If the digits in the tenths place are the same, compare the hundredths place, the second place after the decimal point, and so on. In this case, all the decimals have a zero before the decimal point, so we'll start by comparing the tenths place. 0.55, 0.500, and 0.505 all have a 5 in the tenths place, while 0.0555 has a zero in the tenths place. So, 0.55, 0.500, and 0.505 are larger than 0.0555. Now, compare the hundredths place of the remaining choices, discarding the 0.0555 that we now know is smallest. 0.55 has a 5 in the hundredths place, while 0.500 and 0.505 both have zeroes. So, 0.55 is the largest of the choices.

17. B: To convert a number to scientific notation, move the decimal point until there is just one digit before it (not counting leading zeroes), and rewrite the number as the result times a power of ten. The exponent of the power of ten is equal to the number of places the decimal point was moved—positive if the decimal was moved left, and negative if the decimal was moved right. Starting with 0.05, to put only one digit before the decimal point, we have to move the decimal point two places to the left. Therefore, $0.05 = 5 \times 10^{-2}$, and choices A and C are equal. To convert a percent to a decimal, divide it by 100, which is equivalent to moving the decimal point two places to the left: so $5\% = 0.05$, and choices A and D are equal. However, expressed as a fraction,

$0.05 = \frac{5}{100} = \frac{5 \times 1}{5 \times 20} = \frac{1}{20} \neq \frac{1}{50}$. So choices A, C, and D are equal, but B is not equal to the other three.

ELEMENTARY ALGEBRA

18. D: To solve this problem, all we need to do is substitute -1 for every x in the expression and then simplify: $\frac{2(-1)-2}{(-1)+3} = \frac{-2-2}{2} = \frac{-4}{2} = -2$.

19. B: To simplify the inequality $x^2 + 2x \geq x + 6$, we can first move all the terms to the left-hand side: $x^2 + 2x - x - 6 \geq 0$, which, after combining like terms, becomes $x^2 + x - 6 \geq 0$. We can now factor the left-hand side; since the leading coefficient is 1, one way to do this is to look for two numbers that add to the coefficient of x (here 1) and multiply to the constant term (here -6). The two numbers that qualify are -2 and 3, so $x^2 + x - 6 = (x - 2)(x + 3)$. This makes the inequality $(x - 2)(x + 3) \geq 0$. We know the dividing points for the regions that do and do not satisfy the inequality are then at $x - 2 = 0$ and at $x + 3 = 0$, that is at $x = 2$ and at $x = -3$. Consider the sign in each region: when $x < -3$, then $x - 2$ and $x + 3$ are both negative, and their product is positive. When $-3 < x < 2$, then $x - 2$ is negative and $x + 3$ is positive, so their product is negative. When $x > 2$, then then $x - 2$ and $x + 3$ are both positive, and their product is again positive.

$(x - 2)(x + 3) \geq 0$ when $x \leq -3$ or $x \geq 2$. This is correctly represented by choice B.

20. C: Probably the simplest way to solve this equation is to first get rid of the fractions by multiplying each term by their lowest common denominator, which is $6x$: then we have

$\frac{6x}{2x} + \frac{6x}{x} = \frac{6x}{6}$, which reduces to $3 + 6 = x$. So, $x = 3 + 6 = 9$.

21. B: If there are n floors, and each floor has a height of h feet, then to find the total height of the floors, we just multiply the number of floors by the height of each floor: nh. To find the total height of the building, we must also add the height of the spire, 30 feet. So, the building's total height in feet is $nh + 30$.

22. B: First, let's distribute the x and y that are outside the parentheses and then combine like terms: $(y - 2) + y(3 - x) = (xy - 2x) + (3y - xy) = -2x + 3y + xy - xy = -2x + 3y$.

23. D: Any negative number is less than any positive number, so $-\frac{1}{4}$ must be the first in the list. For numbers with equal numerators, the number with the greater denominator is smaller. So $\frac{1}{5} < \frac{1}{3}$, and $\frac{1}{3} < \frac{1}{1} = 1$. The correct ordering for the given numbers is, therefore, $-\frac{1}{4}, \frac{1}{5}, \frac{1}{3}, 1$.

24. A: The area of a square is equal to the square of the length of its side, or s^2. The area of a triangle is equal to one-half its base times its height, $A = \frac{1}{2}bh$. Here, the base of the triangle is the same as the side of the square, $b = s$, and we are told that its height is three times that of the square, $h = 3s$. In terms of s, the area of the triangle is $A = \frac{1}{2} \times s \times 3s = \frac{3}{2}s^2$. The total area of the figure is then $s^2 + \frac{3}{2}s^2 = \frac{2}{2}s^2 + \frac{3}{2}s^2 = \frac{5}{2}s^2$.

25. D: Use the rule that $(a + b)(a - b) = a^2 - b^2$ or multiply the bionomials using the FOIL method: multiply together the First term of each factor, then the Outer, then the Inner, then the Last, and add the products together.

$(x + 6)(x - 6) = x \times x + x \times (-6) + 6 \times x + 6 \times (-6) = x^2 - 6x + 6x - 36 = x^2 - 36$.

26. D: There are several ways to solve a system of equations like this. One is by substitution. If $x + 2y = 3$, then $x = -2y + 3$. Substituting that into the other equation, $-x - 3y = 4$, we get $-(-2y + 3) - 3y = 4 \Rightarrow 2y - 3 - 3y = 4 \Rightarrow -y - 3 = 4 \Rightarrow -y = 7 \Rightarrow y = -7$. Now, putting that value for y back into one of the original equations, we get $x + 2(-7) = 3 \Rightarrow x - 14 = 3 \Rightarrow x = 17$.

27. B: The average is the total amount spent divided by the number of students. The first three students spend an average of $10, so the total amount they spend is $3 \times \$10 = \$30$. The other six students spend an average of $4, so the total amount they spend is $6 \times \$4 = \$24$. The total amount spent by all nine students is $\$30 + \$24 = \$54$, and the average amount they spend is $\$54 \div 9 = \$6$.

28. B: $-\frac{3}{2}\left(\frac{1}{2}+\frac{1}{3}\right)-\frac{2}{3}\left(\frac{1}{2}-\frac{3}{4}\right)=-\frac{3}{2}\left(\frac{3}{6}+\frac{2}{6}\right)-\frac{2}{3}\left(\frac{2}{4}-\frac{3}{4}\right)=-\frac{3}{2}\left(\frac{5}{6}\right)-\frac{2}{3}\left(-\frac{1}{4}\right)=-\frac{3\times5}{2\times6}+\frac{2\times1}{3\times4}=-\frac{15}{12}+$ $\frac{2}{12}=-\frac{13}{12}$. Finally, to convert this to a mixed number, divide the numerator by the denominator; the quotient is the integer part, and the remainder is the new numerator, while the denominator remains the same. $13\div12=1$ with a remainder of 1, so $-\frac{13}{12}=-1\frac{1}{12}$.

29. C: To solve an equation with an absolute value like $|x^2-2|=x$, we can treat it as two separate cases. If x^2-2 is positive, $|x^2-2|=x^2-2$, and the equation becomes simply $x^2-2=x$, which can be rewritten as the quadratic equation $x^2-x-2=0$. Since the leading coefficient is 1, we can factor this quadratic equation by finding two numbers that add to the coefficient of x (–1) and multiply to the constant term (–2); the two qualifying numbers are 1 and –2, and the equation factors to $(x+1)(x-2)=0$, yielding the solutions $x=-1$ and $x=2$. If x^2-2 is negative, then $|x^2-2|=-(x^2-2)$, and the equation becomes $-(x^2-2)=x$, which we can rewrite as $x^2+x+2=0$. Again, this can be factored, as $(x-1)(x+2)=0$, yielding the two additional solutions $x=1$ and $x=-2$. However, this method of solving equations with an absolute value may result in spurious solutions, so we should check all these solutions in the original equation to make sure that they are genuine. $|1^2-2|=|-1|=1$ and $|2^2-2|=|2|=2$, so $x=1$ and $x=2$ are valid solutions to the equation. However, $|(-1)^2-2|=|-1|=1\neq-1$ and $|(-2)^2-2|=|-2|=2\neq-2$, so $x=-1$ and $x=-2$ are not solutions. The equation has two valid solutions.

COLLEGE-LEVEL MATHEMATICS

30. E: To combine a number of exponential terms, it is generally a good start to convert them to equivalent terms containing the same base. In this case, since two of the terms already have a base of $\sqrt{2}$, it may be easiest to convert them all to that base, using the fact that when an exponential is raised to a power, the exponents are multiplied: $\left(a^b\right)^c=a^{bc}$. So, $2^{\sqrt{2}}=\left(\sqrt{2}^2\right)^{\sqrt{2}}=\sqrt{2}^{2\sqrt{2}}$. The equation then becomes $\sqrt{2}^2\times\sqrt{2}^{2\sqrt{2}}=\left(\sqrt{2}^{\sqrt{2}}\right)^x$, the right-hand side of which simplifies to $\sqrt{2}^{\sqrt{2}x}$. As for the left-hand side, we can simplify it using the fact that when terms of the same base are multiplied, the exponents are added: $a^b\times a^c=a^{b+c}$. So $\sqrt{2}^2\times\sqrt{2}^{2\sqrt{2}}=\sqrt{2}^{2+2\sqrt{2}}$, and we have $\sqrt{2}^{2+2\sqrt{2}}=\sqrt{2}^{\sqrt{2}x}$, which implies $2+2\sqrt{2}=\sqrt{2}x$. Dividing both sides of the equation by $\sqrt{2}$, we obtain $\sqrt{2}+2=x$.

31. E: One way to solve a system of inequalities is to plot both inequalities and see where they overlap. In this case, the first inequality describes the interior of a circle, and the second a half-plane; plotting them both on the same graph produces this:

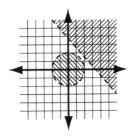

There is no overlap between the shaded areas representing the two inequalities. Therefore, this system of inequalities has no solution.

32. C: The change of base formula for logarithms states that $\log_a x = \frac{\log_b x}{\log_b a}$ for any positive base b. Since $\ln x$ is equivalent to $\log_e x$, we can apply to change of base formula to get $\frac{\ln 81}{\ln 3} = \log_3 81$. $\log_3 81$ can be written as $\log_3 81 = x$, which, by the definition of a logarithm, can be written in standard notation as $3^x = 81$. Since $81 = 3^4$, $\log_3 81 = 4$.

33. D: The quadratic expression $x^2 - 4x + 5$ is not easily factorable, so its roots are best found using the quadratic formula, $x = \frac{-b \pm \sqrt{b^2 - 4ac}}{2a}$. Putting in $a = 1$, $b = -4$, and $c = 5$, this yields $x = \frac{-(-4) \pm \sqrt{(-4)^2 - 4 \times 1 \times 5}}{2 \times 1} = \frac{4 \pm \sqrt{16 - 20}}{2} = \frac{4 \pm \sqrt{-4}}{2} = \frac{4 \pm 2i}{2} = 2 \pm i$.

34. A: This problem is most easily solved using the *law of sines*, which states that the ratio of the sine of each angle in a triangle to the length of the opposite side is equal: $\frac{\sin A}{a} = \frac{\sin B}{b} = \frac{\sin C}{c}$. In this case, angle θ is opposite side a, and the angle with a measure of $30°$ is opposite side b, so we can write $\frac{\sin \theta}{a} = \frac{\sin 30°}{b}$. Since $\sin 30° = \frac{1}{2}$, this becomes $\frac{\sin \theta}{a} = \frac{1/2}{b}$, or $\sin \theta = \frac{a}{2b}$.

35. D: If the two lines intersect at the point $(2, 3)$, that means $x = 2, y = 3$ is a solution to both equations, and we can substitute in those values for x and y to yield $3 = 2a + b$ and $3 = 2b + 2a$. We now have two equations and two unknowns. There are many ways to solve this system of equations, including the substitution method. We can solve the first equation for $2a$ and substitute the result into the second equation, which also contains the term $2a$: the first equation solved for $2a$ is $2a = 3 - b$, and when this value for $2a$ is substituted into the second equation, we can solve for b: $3 = 2b + (3 - b) \Rightarrow 3 = b + 3 \Rightarrow b = 0$. Since we already know $2a = 3 - b$, this means $2a = 3 - 0 = 3$, so $a = \frac{3}{2}$.

36. D: The difference between any two consecutive odd integers is 2. If there are three consecutive odd integers, therefore, and the middle number is x, the other two integers must be $x - 2$ and $x + 2$. So their product is $x(x - 2)(x + 2) = x(x^2 - 4)$ (since $(a - b)(a + b) = a^2 - b^2) = x^3 - 4x$.

37. C: Consider the end behavior of the function. If b were even, then the function would either go to ∞ on both ends or to $-\infty$ on both ends; either way, both ends of the function must be on the same side of the x-axis; therefore, if the function crosses the x-axis, it has to cross it again to get back to the same side as it started. In other words, for an even function, it is impossible for the function to cross the x-axis only once unless the function's maximum or minimum value touched the x-axis, and this scenario is eliminated in the problem. Therefore, b cannot be even, which means b must be odd. (a may be either positive or negative, and c may or may not be zero.)

38. B: Suppose you put the two hosts in two adjacent seats, as required. (It does not matter which two seats we choose since we are not worried about rotations of the whole arrangement.) Then, the other four guests can be arranged in $4! = 4 \times 3 \times 2 \times 1 = 24$ different orders. However, we have to multiply this answer by 2 because there are two possible ways in which the two hosts can be seated; in other words, if they are sitting side-by-side, the hosts can exchange seats and still be sitting together. The total number of orders is $24 \times 2 = 48$.

39. B: The equation $y = 2 \sin(\pi x - \pi)$ can be rewritten as $y = 2 \sin(\pi(x - 1))$. The general form of a sine function is $y = A \sin(B(x - C)) + D$, where the amplitude (the vertical distance from the peak to the center) is $|A|$, the phase shift (horizontal shift) is C, the vertical shift is D, and the period (the width of one full cycle) is $\frac{2\pi}{B}$. In this case, the amplitude is 2, the phase shift is 1, the vertical shift is 0, and the period is $\frac{2\pi}{\pi} = 2$. All of the graphs show the same (correct) amplitude and vertical shift; they only differ in their periods and phase shifts. Consider first the period. The width of one full cycle in the graph is 2 for choices A and B, and 4 for C, D, and E. Since the given function has a period of 2, this means the correct choice must be A or B. Choice A shows what the sine graph would look like without a phase shift: it starts at $x = 0$, then rises to a peak $\frac{1}{4}$ of the way through its period at $x = \frac{2}{4} = \frac{1}{2}$, then crosses the x-axis again halfway through its period at $x = \frac{2}{2} = 1$, and so on. However, the given function has a phase shift of 1, so the entire graph should be shifted right 1 unit. Choice B correctly shows this function.

40. A: If f^{-1} is the inverse of f, then by definition $f^{-1}(f(x)) = x$; therefore, $f\left(f^{-1}(f(x))\right) = f(x) = e^{2x}$.

41. C: The given equation is the standard equation for a plane in three dimensions. More specifically, if a, b, and c are all nonzero, it is a plane not parallel to any of the coordinate axes.

42. D: To simplify this rational expression, we can first factor out the largest common power of x on both sides of the fraction: $\frac{x^7+2x^6+x^5}{x^4-x^2} = \frac{x^5(x^2+2x+1)}{x^2(x^2-1)} = \frac{x^5}{x^2} \times \frac{x^2+2x+1}{x^2-1} = x^3 \times \frac{x^2+2x+1}{x^2-1}$. Now, we can factor both the numerator and denominator of the fraction. The numerator is a quadratic equation that can be factored using the quadratic formula or by other means, but the easiest way to factor it is to recognize it as the square of a binomial: $(a+b)^2 = a^2 + 2ab + b^2$, so $x^2 + 2x + 1 = x^2 + 2(x)(1) + 1^2 = (x+1)^2$. Similarly, the denominator is a difference of squares: $(a+b)(a-b) = a^2 - b^2$, so $x^2 - 1 = x^2 - 1^2 = (x+1)(x-1)$. The expression becomes $x^3 \times \frac{(x+1)^2}{(x+1)(x-1)} = x^3 \times \frac{x+1}{x-1} = \frac{x^3(x+1)}{x-1} = \frac{x^4+x^3}{x-1}$.

43. C: We can write the problem as a system of two linear equations. Let x be the number of gold coins, and y be the number of silver coins. Since there are fifty coins total, we have $x + y = 50$ as one of the equations. If each gold coin weighs 12 ounces, then the total weight in ounces of the gold coins is $12x$; similarly, the total weight in ounces of the silver coins is $8y$. Since all the coins together weigh 30 pounds, which is equal to $30 \times 16 = 480$, we have $12x + 8y = 480$. Because each term in this equation is divisible by 4, we can divide the whole equation by 4 to get $3x + 2y = 120$; this is not a required step, but does make the numbers a little smaller and more manageable.

We now have two equations: $x + y = 50$ and $3x + 2y = 120$. There are a number of ways to solve a system of equations like this. One is to the substitution method. We can solve the first equation for y to get $y = 50 - x$, and then substitute this into the second equation to get $3x + 2(50 - x) = 120$. After distributing the 2, we get $3x + 100 - 2x = 120$; combining like terms gives $x + 100 = 120$, and, finally, subtracting 100 from both sides yields $x = 20$. Therefore, the number of gold coins is 20.

44. D: The standard form of the equation of an ellipse is $\frac{x^2}{a^2} + \frac{y^2}{b^2} = 1$, where a and b are the lengths of the semimajor and semiminor axes—that is, half the lengths of the major and minor axes. The major axis is the longer axis, while the minor axis is the shorter. To put the equation $3x^2 + 4y^2 = 48$ in standard form, we have to divide both sides of the equation by 48: $\frac{3x^2}{48} + \frac{4y^2}{48} = \frac{48}{48} \Rightarrow \frac{x^2}{16} + \frac{y^2}{12} = 1 \Rightarrow \frac{x^2}{4^2} + \frac{y^2}{(2\sqrt{3})^2} = 1$. The lengths of the semimajor and semiminor axes are 4 and $2\sqrt{3}$, and the lengths of our major and minor axes are $2(4) = 8$ and $2(2\sqrt{3}) = 4\sqrt{3}$. Since $8 > 4\sqrt{3}$, the length of the major axis is 8.

45. A: A geometric sequence is a sequence in which the ratio between any two consecutive terms is the same; this ratio is called the *common factor*. The nth term of a geometric sequence with first term a_1 and common factor r is $a_1 r^{n-1}$. In this case, the first term is 80 and the common factor is $\frac{120}{80} = \frac{3}{2}$, so the tenth term is $80 \times \left(\frac{3}{2}\right)^{10-1} = \frac{80}{1} \times \left(\frac{3}{2}\right)^9 = \frac{80 \times 3^9}{2^9} = \frac{2^4 \times 5 \times 3^9}{2^4 \times 2^5} = \frac{5 \times 3^9}{2^5}$.

46. E: If $h(x) = f(x) + g(x)$, then $h(3) = f(3) + g(3)$. $f(3) = e^{3-3} = e^0 = 1$, and

$g(3) = 2 \times 3 - 1 = 6 - 1 = 5$, so $h(3) = 1 + 5 = 6$.

47. E: The simplest way to solve this problem is to first use the trigonometric identity

$\sec^2 \theta = \tan^2 \theta + 1$, or $\tan^2 \theta = \sec^2 \theta - 1$. Replacing $\tan^2 \theta$ with $\sec^2 \theta - 1$, the given equation becomes $2 \sec \theta = \sec^2 \theta - 1$. Moving everything to one side of the equation, we get $\sec^2 \theta - 2 \sec \theta - 1 = 0$. If we let $x = \sec \theta$, this is a simple quadratic equation, $x^2 - 2x - 1 = 0$. We can solve this using the quadratic formula, $= \frac{-b \pm \sqrt{b^2 - 4ac}}{2a}$. In this case, $= \frac{-(-2) \pm \sqrt{(-2)^2 - 4(1)(-1)}}{2(1)} = \frac{2 \pm \sqrt{4-(-4)}}{2} = \frac{2 \pm \sqrt{8}}{2} = \frac{2 \pm 2\sqrt{2}}{2} = 1 \pm \sqrt{2}$. So, $\sec \theta = 1 \pm \sqrt{2}$.

48. C: If the town's population triples every ten years, this is an example of *exponential growth*, which is described by the equation $P = P_0 e^{kt}$, where P is the population at time t, P_0 is the initial population, and k is growth rate. To find k, we can use the fact that ten years after 1950 the town's population will be three times what it started with: i.e., when $t = 10$, $P = 3P_0$. So, $3P_0 = P_0 e^{10k}$; we can cancel out the P_0 from both sides to get $3 = e^{10k}$. Taking the natural logarithm of both sides, we get $\ln 3 = 10k$, so $k = \frac{1}{10} \ln 3$. So our exponential growth equation is $P(t) = P_0 e^{\left(\frac{1}{10} \ln 3\right)t} = P_0 e^{\ln 3 \left(\frac{t}{10}\right)}$; using the fact that $a^{bc} = (a^b)^c$, we can rewrite this as $P(t) = P_0 \left(e^{\ln 3}\right)^{\frac{t}{10}}$. But e^x and $\ln x$ are inverse functions, so $e^{\ln 3} = 3$, and this becomes $P(t) = P_0 \times 3^{\frac{t}{10}}$.

As an alternate way of solving the problem, we can just plug in $t = 10$ to each equation and see which one then yields the proper value of $P(10) = 3P_0$. Respectively, the five choices give $P(10) = 10 P_0^{30}, P_0^3, 3P_0, P_0 \times \left(\frac{3}{10}\right)^{10}$, and $\left(\frac{3}{10} P_0\right)^{10}$; only choice C yields the correct answer.

49. B: A property of inverse functions important for this problem is that if $f(x) = y$, then $f^{-1}(y) = x$. Therefore, from the given information that $f(1) = 2$, $g(2) = 3$, $f^{-1}(3) = 4$, and $g^{-1}(4) = 1$, it also follows that $f^{-1}(2) = 1$, $g^{-1}(3) = 2$, $f(4) = 3$, and $g(1) = 4$. So $f(g(1)) = f(4) = 3$, and choice A is true. $g(f^{-1}(2)) = g(1) = 4$, and choice C is true. $g^{-1}(f^{-1}(3)) = g^{-1}(4) = 1$, and choice D is true. $g(2) = 3 = f(4)$, and choice E is true. The only choice that does *not* follow from the given information is choice B; since we do not know the value of $g(3)$, we cannot determine the value of $f(g(3))$.

Thank You

We at Mometrix would like to extend our heartfelt thanks to you, our friend and patron, for allowing us to play a part in your journey. It is a privilege to serve people from all walks of life who are unified in their commitment to building the best future they can for themselves.

The preparation you devote to these important testing milestones may be the most valuable educational opportunity you have for making a real difference in your life. We encourage you to put your heart into it—that feeling of succeeding, overcoming, and yes, conquering will be well worth the hours you've invested.

We want to hear your story, your struggles and your successes, and if you see any opportunities for us to improve our materials so we can help others even more effectively in the future, please share that with us as well. **The team at Mometrix would be absolutely thrilled to hear from you!** So please, send us an email (support@mometrix.com) and let's stay in touch.

If you feel as though you need additional help, please check out the other resources we offer:

> Study Guide: http://MometrixStudyGuides.com/ACCUPLACER
>
> Flashcards: http://MometrixFlashcards.com/ACCUPLACER